33031

Humes, James C.

PN
4121
H8.57

Roles speakers
pley

OCT 23 84 77

D1006492

LEARNING RESOURCE CENTER
Fort Steilacoom
Community College
Tacoma, WA 98458

ROLES SPEAKERS PLAY

BOOKS BY JAMES C. HUMES

Roles Speakers Play

Podium Humor

Instant Eloquence

LEARNING RESOURCE CENTER
Fort Steilaccom
Community College
Tacoma, WA 98498

ROLES
SPEAKERS PLAY

James C. Humes

HARPER & ROW, PUBLISHERS

NEW YORK

HAGERSTOWN

SAN FRANCISCO

LONDON

1817

33031

ROLES SPEAKERS PLAY. Copyright © 1976 by James C. Humes. All rights reserved. Printed in the United States of America. No part of this book may be used or reproduced in any manner whatsoever without written permission except in the case of brief quotations embodied in critical articles and reviews. For information address Harper & Row, Publishers, Inc., 10 East 53rd Street, New York, N.Y. 10022. Published simultaneously in Canada by Fitzhenry & Whiteside Limited, Toronto.

FIRST EDITION

Designed by Sidney Feinberg

Library of Congress Cataloging in Publication Data

Humes, James C
  Roles speakers play.
  Includes indexes.
  1. Public speaking. I. Title.
PN4121.H857   808.5'1   75-25042
ISBN 0-06-012003-7

76 77 78 79 10 9 8 7 6 5 4 3 2 1

To Sam, who has played the role of big brother
both as father and friend

Contents

Acknowledgments

Just a note in expression of thanks and appreciation to Stephanie Laszlo, who typed and corrected each page as it was drafted, and to Bill Davies, who read and edited each chapter as it was received in New York.

I am much indebted to the patience and understanding of both.

PART I: ROLES OF
THE SPEAKER

CHAPTER 1

The Speaker and His Seven Roles

"One man in his time plays many parts."
SHAKESPEARE, *As You Like It*

Shakespeare wrote, "And one man in his time plays many parts, His acts being seven ages." There are also seven roles of a speaker. If man must play the part of infant, schoolboy, lover, soldier, father, old man, second childhood, a speaker has different roles: advocate, lecturer, commemorator, toastmaker, moderator, introducer, honoree. Each role has its own format, its own style.

A cornerstone-laying speech is different from a campaign talk. The presentation of a travelogue is not the same as that of a sales pitch. You would not introduce a speaker in the same way you would toast the father of the bride.

British Prime Minister William Gladstone used to keep five desks in his house—his desk as Prime Minister, his desk as head of the Liberal party, his desk as an author, his desk for personal correspondence, and his desk for business affairs.

When he sat in each place, he assumed a different role. At his living-room desk he played the statesman, but in his downstairs study he thought as a political partisan. When he wanted to write to friends, he went to the upstairs study, but when he felt like penning another chapter to his latest book, he would go to the library. Or, if he had to settle some household bills, he went to the room off the pantry. In each he played a different part —Prime Minister, party leader, writer, friend, or head of house.

It is the same way for a speech. Sometimes you are a teacher;

other times you are a salesman. If you have to give an invocation, you become a preacher. But, when you give a toast, you have to act the role of entertainer.

Another Prime Minister, Winston Churchill, used to imagine himself in different hats and uniforms. There were the top hat and morning clothes he wore to state functions as the King's first minister. When he would go to the House of Commons from 10 Downing Street, he would wear his homburg, bow tie and vest. While painting, he wore his smock along with a wide-brimmed hat. For writing, he would don the famous zippered siren suit he designed himself. When he was making army inspections, he would wear his peaked officer's hat with military-style overcoat. Then there was the favorite he would use to pose for great royal occasions—his cocked hat and braided and bemedaled uniform as Warden of the Cinque Ports.

Don't we sometimes pick a tie and suit to fit the occasion of our appearance? If it is a eulogy or memorial service, we choose a dark suit and a somber tie. But if we are the birthday celebrant we may wear a tie in festive red or perhaps a gaudy waistcoat. When the Rotary Club asks you to speak as head of this year's United Fund drive, you go for the gray suit and conservative regimental-striped tie.

The Stanislavsky method of acting demands that actors and actresses do more than think the role—they should actually live the part. Well, you don't have to become a minister to give a sermon or a comedian to emcee a gridiron dinner, but just try imagining yourself in such a role. Think of how you would handle the following situations: making a sales pep talk, delivering a eulogy at a memorial service for a deceased judge or a closing summation to the jury, chairing a political debate for the Chamber of Commerce, toasting your aunt at a golden wedding anniversary reception, acting as toastmaster for the Press Club gridiron dinner, testifying for the new bond referendum before the city council, accepting the Association's Man of the Year award, or introducing the Governor.

In all of these speech appearances how would you see yourself: leader, friend, expert? How would you be dressed: formal or casual? What would be your decorum: purposeful or relaxed? What would be your speaking style: matter-of-fact or breezy?

Although the variety of speech occasions seems unlimited, there are actually only seven roles to play. It is like the first time I was asked to speak as a newly-elected state legislator from upstate Pennsylvania. Flattered by the attentions of the nearby county politicos, I wanted to give a brilliant oration at the Lincoln Day Republican Dinner. I asked the local county chairman if it would be all right if my title was "Whither the Republican Party—Reaction or Reform?" He said, "Humes, you can speak on anything you want as long as you're against the gun-control bill, against the Supreme Court decision on school prayers—and against Philadelphia."

Well, similarly, no matter whether you see yourself as young legislator or old professor, country preacher or city leader, public official or proud father, there are still only seven ways of doing a speech—as advocate, lecturer, commemorator, toastmaker, moderator, introducer, or honoree.

How do you tell which category your speech is going to fit into? Easy—just figure out the purpose of your appearance. Are you going to sell a proposal? Explain a concept? Memorialize an occasion? Salute a friend? Chair a panel? Present a speaker? Or thank your associates?

When you have to *sell* a bond proposal you become an advocate. As an advocate, you are speaking *for* something or someone—either a cause or a candidate.

If you are asked to *explain* a concept like Zen Buddhism, you are a lecturer, or teacher. If you give a Bicentennial talk on Philadelphia in the Revolution or an account of your recent trip to China, you are playing the role of lecturer. The difference between being an advocate and being a lecturer is the difference between "exhorting" and "explaining." The test is whether you are getting the audience to take action or just giving them the benefit of your expertise. Are you an investment banker whose speech title is "Municipal Authorities and City Finance"? Or are you a civic leader whose speech subject is "Vote Yes on the Park Bond Referendum"?

In my first campaign for the legislature, I went literally door to door, knocking at every home during my campaign to upset a six-term incumbent. In some of the homes I was asked in and given a cup of coffee by the housewife. At one of the Republican dinners where my opponent and I each had to make an appearance, I noticed one of the women who had seemed particularly hospitable to me working at a booth manned by the opposition. Recalling her warm interest in the conversation we had had over her kitchen table about my education and qualifications, I was somewhat surprised as well as disappointed. "Well," I said as I went over to greet her, "You know I hoped you would be working for me." "But, Mr. Humes," she replied, "you never asked me to."

So just remember, if you are an advocate trying to sell yourself or your program, make sure you ask the audience to do something—vote, contribute, pass a resolution, or write their Congressman.

Of course, if you are only appearing as a lecturer or teacher you don't have to request the audience to take action. Neither does a commemorator ask for adoption of a concrete proposal or program. He may, however, invite his listeners to share with him a feeling, a remembrance, an awareness, or an appreciation. The difference between the commemorator and the lecturer is mainly this: the lecturer works with facts but the commemorator tends to deal in feelings.

The role of a commemorator looks easy. But it is a role that most speakers stumble over—because expressing feelings is far more difficult than explaining facts. As a lawyer you might have no trouble working up remarks urging a woman's group to make sure they and their husbands write wills. You could also talk about your own specialty of estate work. But what if you have to deliver a courtroom address welcoming newly naturalized citizens? This is a moving moment for the immigrant families. A legal description of the duties of citizenship is not enough. You must as a commemorator capture the drama of the event.

If you rise to the occasion you will give a talk that will be remembered long after your talk on writing a will or estate planning will be forgotten.

Remember, the greatest speeches ever delivered were commemorative addresses—Lincoln's Gettysburg Address, Pericles' Funeral Oration. An advocate may be compelling, a lecturer may be fascinating, but there is a certain poignancy in a eulogy or dedication that can make the commemorator truly eloquent.

Of course, eulogies and memorial dedications are not the only commemorative talks. An Eagle Scout award ceremony, a retirement dinner, a Veteran's Day observance are all occasions for the commemorator. They seem simple enough—in fact, so simple that the speaker frequently doesn't prepare beforehand. The result is that the would-be commemorator plods through a series of banalities, turning a festive occasion into a bore.

Like the commemorator, the toastmaker deals with sentiments. The difference is that the toast is always bright and happy. It is also shorter than a memorializing speech. A five-minute or shorter talk, it is a personal salute to a person or an institution.

When we think of a toast, we mostly think of a fun occasion, such as a wedding, christening, or bon voyage party. But there are also the more formal varieties required in official or state functions.

Right after World War I the French hero Marshal Foch was in this country on a speaking tour. At a dinner party in Denver, he raised his glass to toast President Warren Harding. Later, a guest came up to him and said, "Don't you think this diplomatic protocol of offering toasts is really a lot of hot air?"

"Yes," he replied, "they are like the hot air in a pneumatic tire but they smooth out the bumps in life's highway."

To smooth out bumps is a good way of describing the role of a moderator too. The job of a moderator is to keep things running smoothly. Whether he is presiding over a panel, or emceeing a banquet he is the on-stage production manager. He has to make sure all the presentations or speeches tie together. He is the "bridger" from one speaker to the next.

Not long ago a classmate of my ten-year-old daughter said, "One thing my Mom is really great at—no matter what you're talking about she can turn the subject to schoolwork. The other day I asked her about having a slumber party and she said, 'Do you talk over your homework assignments at those parties?' "

A good moderator has to be just as inventive. Not only must he know what the background of each speaker is but he also must keep notes on what each of them has to say. In that way he is able to connect the speeches of the various panelists. The moderator then is not so much a speaker as a splicer. He splices together the personalities and presentations of the program.

Another variation of the moderator is the master of ceremonies. Because humor is the stuff of his splicing the emcee is like a moderator in party clothes. Adlai Stevenson once described the role of an emcee as that of a fan dancer—to cover the subject only enough to make it tantalizing.

The fan-dance comparison could be a definition of any good introduction. An example of the bad introduction may be that of the Texan who was to present Lord Balfour, Britain's Foreign Secretary at a rally in World War I. Instead of offering a brief sketch of the British statesman he gave a forty-minute thesis summarizing the causes of the war—and then almost as an afterthought he said, "Now Lord Balfour will give his address." Lord Balfour rose and said, "I'm supposed to give my address in the brief time remaining. Here it is: 10 Carleton Gardens, London, England."

The lawyer Louis Nizer, who has made an art form of the speaker presentation, once described the introducer as a "teller of little stories." The introduction is not so much a little lecture as a little biography. In the span of two or three minutes you must paint the life of the speaker or the institution he has built, or the cause he represents. I say "paint" because it should be more an impressionistic picture than a statistical graph.

Sometimes a speaker may find it hard to live up to a powerful introduction. But he soon learns that a few self-deprecating lines serve as an antidote to the extended compliment. What is really difficult is to have to give a whole speech in response to praise. That is why the honoree—be he retiring president or victorious candidate—should give some thought beforehand to preparing his acceptance speech.

Lord Chesterfield once wrote to his son, "Gratitude is a burden upon our imperfect nature." In other words, Chesterfield was instructing his boy, learn how to say thank you. If feelings are more difficult to express than fact, feelings of gratitude are the most difficult of all. The role of the honoree is to turn the focus of attention on himself back to his audience or to those in the audience who have done most to bring him to the position of honor he holds on this occasion. But he has to do it in a way that is not awkward but graceful.

Just because most acceptance speeches seem impromptu does not excuse lack of preparation. You must frame your words of appreciation in a way that doesn't demean you or diminish your friends. They must be made part of your success.

Once President Calvin Coolidge, while on a whistle-stop tour, was summoned by a distraught aide to greet a group of well-wishers. They had come to cheer outside his presidential car, which was resting in an overnight siding. The pajama-clad President came to the rear platform and looking around said, "This crowd is too big for an anecdote and too small for an oration."

Coolidge should have been honored by the outpouring of affection and at least thanked the group. Or he could have assumed the role of advocate and delivered a short campaign pep talk. With every audience there is the right role for the speaker to play. Make sure you know beforehand whether you are going to be advocate, lecturer, commemorator, toastmaker, moderator, introducer, or honoree.

CHAPTER 2

The Speaker as Advocate

"The humblest citizen of all the land, when clad in
the armor of a righteous cause, is stronger than all
the hosts of Error."

WILLIAM JENNINGS BRYAN

One of the top TV newsmen in Philadelphia told me how he
was instructing a young girl who was interested in doing television work. The girl's problem was shyness. He told her: "Look,
most actors and actresses are shy. That's why acting appeals so
much to them. They are not being themselves on stage; they are
playing a role. So when you are on camera, play a role, assume
a different personality. I know newsmen who started out playing David Brinkley or Walter Cronkite until they shaped their
own style—one that they were comfortable with."

It is the same in speaking. You play different roles in being
an advocate and being a lecturer. When you think of an advocate you think of a lawyer. Can't you picture a courtroom, the
lawyer with his open briefcase beside him? There he is arguing
to the jury that the airline had a duty to keep the pathway to
the airplane steps free from an oil slick on which his client
slipped. Can't you visualize in your mind what the attorney
would be wearing?

That doesn't mean that if you are going to the Rotary Club
to speak in favor of a new no-fault auto insurance bill you have
to wear a pinstriped suit, striped tie, and horn-rimmed glasses.
But you would dress differently than you would going to the
club's annual stag evening affair. The advocate dresses in simple

bold lines. He is sure of himself, sure of his facts, and sure of his client's innocence or of his bill's validity. He does not show insecurity by adopting the trendiest fashion in clothes. There is an aura about him of bold simplicity. The lawyer often looks as if clothes were not a major concern. But, if you look closely, you may suspect that that conservative suit is tailor-made.

In somewhat the same way the lawyer picks his facts. He seems to be giving you all the facts in a fair, balanced presentation, but actually he is only giving those facts that strengthen his side.

When Henry Kissinger was Special Assistant to President Nixon on National Security Affairs, he used to say, "I don't tell the President what he *should* do, I tell him what he *can* do—the various options and the pros and cons of each option." "Yes, Henry," said his critics, "but you weigh the options in favor of what you think he should do."

The lawyer may sketchily summarize the argument of the opposition so that he may easily dismiss it. The lawyer is a debater—he is persuading you to his side of the argument. As an advocate you have to do the same. When I was a young lawyer, I argued a case as a public defender and lost. Afterward a senior lawyer criticized my handling of the case. "Humes," he said, "you were too fair. Your job is not to be judge but advocate. You are not supposed to be objective—only *seem* to be objective."

In 1933 the newly elected President Franklin Roosevelt went across Pennsylvania Avenue from the White House to call on the ninety-year-old Justice Holmes. "Mr. Justice," said Roosevelt, "your life has covered more than half the history of this republic. What advice can you give me?"

"Mr. President," replied Holmes, "you are in a warlike crisis. In that situation you must marshal resources and fight."

The Anglo-American court system is based on the "adversary" principle—truth emerges in the conflict between plaintiff and defendant or rather between the plaintiff's lawyer and the defendant's lawyer.

If you are proposing a national health-insurance program,

you are fighting the AMA. If you are supporting no-fault divorce, you may be combating certain lay leaders in the Catholic Church. Whatever legislation or program you are advocating, you can be sure there are important interests opposing you or else the program would have already been adopted. Don't worry about giving only one side of the picture. The other side will demand "equal representation" or "their day in court." You are not a referee but a participant. As long as you don't lie, you are being fair.

Old Sam Ervin tells of advice he received as a young North Carolina lawyer. "If the facts are on your side, appeal to the jury's minds, if emotions are running in your favor, appeal to their hearts, and if you don't have either, just bang the table and shout."

Well, you won't have to bang any table or podium because, unlike a lawyer, you don't have to argue a position in which you have little faith. You may not have the lawyer's skills in argument, but you have something better—belief in the truth of your own cause. As William Jennings Bryan said, a man "clad in the armour of a righteous cause, is mightier than all the hosts of Error." Whether you are arguing for a city-manager form of government or legalization of marijuana, you believe you are fighting for an "idea whose time has come." Think of Émile Zola fighting to vindicate Captain Dreyfus. Anatole France said Zola's advocacy was better than that of any lawyer. He was, said France at Zola's funeral, "a moment in the conscience of history." Any time you speak to fight injustice or aid humanity, you can be "a moment in the conscience of history."

You see, you don't have to be a lawyer to fight for a cause. But it helps to think and act like one. Brief yourself on *all* the facts and then choose those that help your side the most.

As a lawyer ponders the jury he will face, and considers the arguments that will most sway them, you must assess the group you will speak to.

I heard a legislator argue to a black audience that "forced busing" was a kind of racism since it implied that black children could only learn when associating with whites. And I listened to a feminist say to a Kiwanis audience that the Equal Rights Amendment would free divorced men from the injustice of alimony.

But, whatever your audience, your first task as advocate is to get the attention of the audience. You do that by telling a story —not a funny story but a life experience, perhaps a personal human tragedy that exemplifies the problem your program is going to solve.

This technique is not new. In fact, it is part of the E.A.S.E. formula I advocated in my book *Instant Eloquence* in 1973. But I see no reason to change. John Kennedy once resisted a legislative amendment citing the rule of the English statesman Lord Falkland. "When it is not necessary to change, it is necessary *not* to change."

My acronym in 1973 was E.A.S.E. *(exemplify, amplify, specify, electrify)*. And in the advocacy type of speech it is still the best formula for inciting an audience to action.

First, you open your speech with a life example. You don't talk about abstractions like inflation or pollution. You hold up a supermarket advertisement from five years ago and then route your expedition into that same supermarket yesterday. Or you describe two dead fish you saw washed ashore in your favorite trout stream.

The author Charles Kingsley once asked the seascapist Turner how he painted his famous picture of a storm at sea.

Turner replied, "I wished to paint a storm at sea. So I went to the coast of Holland and engaged a fisherman to take me out in his boat in the next storm. The storm was brewing and I went down to his boat and asked him to bind me to its mast. Then he drove the boat out into the teeth of the storm. The storm was so furious that I longed to be down in the bottom of the boat and allow it to blow over me. But I could not; I was bound to the mast. Not only did I see the storm and feel it, but it blew itself into me till I became part of the storm. And then I came back and painted the picture."

You want to make your audience part of the storm by painting a picture. You want to make them see and feel the problem too. If you are advocating a new health-insurance program, paint a picture of a man whose home, property, and life savings are dissipated in one costly operation. If at all possible, choose the story of a man you know or one you've heard about.

In 1965 I headed a committee in my state's bar association to push for the adoption of a new constitutional amendment for presidential succession. (One of the provisions least debated was that for selecting a Vice President when that office was vacant. Little did we realize that, in a few years, Ford and Rockefeller would be chosen that way.) The amendment, which was later ratified, provided for orderly succession in case of presidential disability. So, in the speech I delivered to various Rotary, Kiwanis, and Grange organizations around the state, I opened my talk with a description from history—James Garfield lying in a coma, incapacitated by an assassin's bullet for eighty-two days. The Presidency was paralyzed; various government activities ground to a halt. In 1965 hardly a year since John Kennedy's assassination, it was easy to paint the national horror if Kennedy had not died from the rifle shot but had lived on in a coma.

Any advocacy address states a problem and a solution to that problem. So you must open your speech by "exemplifying" that problem in graphic, dramatic terms.

I heard Dick Sprague, the noted prosecutor of the Yablonski murder case, once speak out against the Warren Court decisions inhibiting law enforcement. He started his speech by sketching the details of a grisly rape of a young hospital intern. The rapist, who had a prior record, was tried and convicted. He appealed and won—even though the arrest, interrogation, and conduct of trial were deemed proper. He won it because the judge said upon leaving the courtroom, "May God guide you in your deliberations." The State Supreme Court voided the trial because "God had been called in as a thirteenth juror." Thirteen months later the same accused raped and killed a twelve-year-old girl.

Not all of us have such vivid crime stories at our fingertips. But you can easily find one with a phone call to the District

Attorney's office or a visit to a public library. When I was asked to give a speech on crime prevention, I found a story in a recent *Newsweek* issue with a special report on crime.

> She was one of those shapeless, faceless old women who live out their lives in the anonymity of the inner city. Her home was a cheap hotel in San Francisco's sleazy Tenderloin. Her friends were the other tenants who gathered in the lobby to watch TV. Her exercise was the short walk to a local cafeteria for meals. Then she was mugged in the street one night, knocked down and robbed, and an almost visible pall of fear enveloped her. For days she sat rooted in the lobby, suspicious even of the regulars. Finally, she retreated to her own room. When old friends tried to visit her she refused to open the door lest an intruder somehow slip in. For a fortnight, nobody saw her at all and a worried desk clerk finally went upstairs to check. There she lay, sprawled on the floor, dead for a week. The official reports said she had died of a perforated "stress ulcer" complicated by malnutrition. What she really died of was fear.

Sometimes you have to find your "exemplifying" opener out of history or literature. Once when I was ghosting a speech on consumer legislation for a U.S. Senator, I began the speech draft with this description of sixteenth-century Czechoslovakia:

> In the center of Prague before Hradcany Castle you will find a well. It is not an ordinary well but a cage well—the cage could hold those who cheated buyers. In that well, fraudulent butchers, bakers and other merchants who cheated on their weights or prices were dunked upside down in a public ceremony under an edict of King Wenceslas.

For a speech on welfare reform I lifted this example from Japanese literature:

> In a Japanese novel of several years ago the main character, wandering in a strange village, becomes trapped at the bottom of a sand pit. Food and water are lowered to him but no ladder. He wants out desperately. He begs his captors to let him go. He tries to bargain with them, but nothing works. Months pass. The begging becomes a way of life.
> After a long time he is granted what he wants—freedom. Sud-

denly he is afraid. He doesn't want freedom—he is hooked on his dependency.

Now that you have focused on the problem by "exemplifying," you continue by "amplifying" on it. It's like the answer the early union organizer Samuel Gompers gave in response to a question. "Mr. Gompers," he was asked, "when you get an eight-hour day, what will be your goal then?" "More," he replied. "More what?" was the next question. "More wages, more holidays, more benefits." So, once you have dramatized the problem for the audience, you must drive the point home by expanding on it—by describing the other implications.

If you're talking about welfare reform, you will then discuss the effect increasing welfare rolls has in bankrupting the city treasury, robbing the city of other needed services, or contributing to the disintegration of the family, as well as discouraging individual initiative.

Or suppose, in arguing for a new environmental code, you "exemplified" the problem of pollution with the finding of the bloated dead fish in the upstate stream. Then to "amplify" you will want to detail the other dangers of pollution—the waste of water supply, the killing of natural wild life, the spread of disease in addition to the closing down of recreational sports like swimming and fishing.

Not long ago I heard a Democratic Governor announce his campaign for the Presidency in this way. First he "exemplified" Ford as a latter-day Herbert Hoover for his handling of the New York City financial crisis. Then he "amplified" by attacking the other figures of the Ford Cabinet—former Secretary of State Kissinger for secret wheeling-dealing, Secretary of Treasury Simon for being the tool of Wall Street, and Secretary of Agriculture Butz for selling out the consumer in favor of big business.

In that respect, the Governor reminded me of Pooh-Bah in Gilbert and Sullivan's *Mikado:* "I've got a little list" of people "who never would be missed." In a way, the "amplify" part of the speech is a list just as the "exemplify" part is a story.

Let's say that you are advocating the abolition of the electoral college. Your notes might look like this:

Exemplify: Case of Samuel Tilden who "lost" to Rutherford Hayes in 1876 despite the fact that he received more popular votes.

Amplify: A. Undemocratic.
             B. Members of Electoral College can be arbitrary in their selection notwithstanding votes of their constituency.
             C. Unhealthy influence of big states with many electoral votes.

You can see that "exemplify" often means a dramatic case history and "amplify" often is a list of reasons why a change is necessary.

During the Revolutionary War one of the most controversial members of the British Parliament was John Wilkes. Wilkes, who supported the American cause, was hated by the Tories. His rebelliousness and roguish charms might have endeared him to the ladies and his London constituency but it made him anathema to the Tory front bench. At one time Lord Sandwich confronted Wilkes and said, "The honourable gentleman will have a limited career in this chamber for it shall either end on the gallows or by some loathsome social disease." The irrepressible Wilkes replied, "The honourable Lord may be correct in his prediction. It all depends on whether I embrace his program or his mistress."

Advocates as well as politicians should have programs to put forth. That is the solution they "specify." In any advocacy speech you are endorsing a bill, submitting a plan, promoting a product, or backing a candidate. Once you have "exemplified" a problem and "amplified" on the reasons why it needs to be dealt with, then you have to "specify" a solution.

When I was in the State Department, I was once asked to draft a speech for Secretary Rogers on the missing POWs. The Secretary's office sent me an outline of the necessary facts. But missing from the staff paper was any proposal as to what people could do about it. In other words the paper was a detailed analysis of the problem with no recommendation for solution. I questioned the use of a major forum for a speech that invited frustration instead of suggesting an action to be taken. I argued for asking people to write the International Red Cross or appropriate officials in the U.S. They told me that such an action would be a futile gesture. I replied, "If you don't tell the people something they can do that might lead to a return of some of the prisoners, that doesn't make a full-fledged speech. You are not saying anything more than the answers in a press conference would reveal."

In an advocacy speech you have to do more than outline a problem. You must offer a program—a bill to be passed, a referendum to be satisfied, or an item to be included in the budget.

Today we hear many Congressmen talk about crime and yet offer no constructive program to combat it. They feel it sufficient to rail at the Supreme Court and lenient judges. Let's for example see how a speech on crime would shape up in notes:

Exemplify: Story about old woman whose death was medically attributed to ulcers and malnutrition but was really caused by stark terror.

Amplify: A. Increase in city and suburban crimes; rapes and muggings.
B. Revolving-door justice of convicted rapists and muggers being released.
C. Many crimes done by repeaters while out on bail.

Specify: Federal anti-crime package.
1. Constitutional amendment allowing capital punishment.
2. Constitutional amendment for elimination of bail for repeaters.
3. Mandatory Federal sentences for bank robbers.

The German poet Heinrich Heine was once asked how the medieval Germans ever built those lofty cathedrals. Heine replied, "Men in those days had more than just an opinion, they felt a commitment."

So an advocate should do more than persuade his audience of the righteousness of his cause; he should persuade them to do something about it—to send letters to their Congressmen, to contribute their fair share to the United Fund, to pass a resolution of their civic club to be forwarded to the Mayor's office.

My mother used to criticize certain Presbyterian ministers. After a particularly bland Sunday-morning sermon, she would say, "He only told us to be good—we all know that. He should ask us to do something this week like visiting a sick person, or calling a long-out-of-touch relative. He can't just say 'Love our fellow man'—that's nothing we can get our teeth into." Similarly, you want to "electrify" your audience into doing something. You should try to turn the audience on—turn them from passive listeners to active participants. You should get them out of their seats—to canvass their blocks for a candidate, solicit the street for the heart drive, or pledge their check for the building fund.

In electricity you plug things in. To "electrify" the audience you must plug the audience in—to the action. Tell them what their role or part is. The U.S. agency ACTION has a slogan: "If you're not part of the solution, you're part of the problem." That is what "electrifying" the audience is all about: it is recruiting the audience to be part of the solution.

In the E.A.S.E. formula you explain the problem by exemplifying it and then amplifying on it. Then you offer the solution by specifying a program, then electrifying or sparking audience participation.

In 1953 Winston Churchill, while traveling to the United States on the *Queen Mary,* asked his scientific adviser Lord Cherwell to figure out how much liquor he had consumed in his lifetime and whether it would fill the main salon. Lord Cherwell took out his slide rule and retired to his cabin. Hours later

Cherwell came back and said, "If all the wine, brandy, and whisky you have drunk in your lifetime was poured into this salon, it comes right up to eye-level." Churchill replied, "When I look up at the ceiling and contemplate my seventy-nine years, I can only say, 'How much left to do and how little time to do it.'"

If only you can end your speech on a similar note of immediacy and urgency, you will be an "electrifying" success. You can, if you build your advocacy speech on the E.A.S.E. formula.

CHAPTER 3

The Speaker as Lecturer

> "The man who can make hard things easy is the educator."
>
> RALPH WALDO EMERSON

In his movie *Paper Chase,* John Houseman conveys a powerful impression of a Harvard Law professor. The burly tweed-jacketed academician may be just like the rest of us as a father or a host in his own home but in the classroom he is utterly sure of himself—because he has mastered his field of law.

You know why college professors are so casual in their clothes —the patched tweed coat, the old pullover, the creaseless flannels? Because they don't have to prove anything. A men's fashion consultant recently wrote that businessmen wanting to be successful must try to look successful, in blue pin-striped three-piece suits. But he added that the academician, unless he is college president or vice president for alumni relations, doesn't have to impress anyone. Why? Because when he strides to the head of the classroom he is boss, however he dresses.

But no matter how absent-minded he seems to be about his appearance, he is all business about his specialty—be it ancient history or modern literature. The teacher we remember twenty years later is the one whose enthusiasm for the Roman republic made Cicero's speech against Catiline as exciting as Watergate or one whose reading of Dylan Thomas made Bob Dylan seem pale by comparison.

To an audience a good lecturer is more than a teacher—he is a guide, a veteran explorer who takes his listeners hand in hand through new cultures and antique lands. But to play the role of lecturer you don't have to be an Einstein of physics or a Galbraith in economics; you only have to feel that you know more about your speech topic than anyone else in the audience. You don't have to persuade the audience of your point of view like an advocate; you only have to persuade them that you are an expert.

An expert was once described as a stranger from the next town with a starched shirt, a shoe shine, and a briefcase. It is much easier to be an expert in a strange town than in your own home town. When I speak in Williamsport, Pennsylvania, I am still Jamie Humes, who at the age of six tried to learn to ride a bike down the steepest hill while reading a book, and ended up with a telephone pole breaking my ribs. But when I go across the country lecturing, I am James Calhoun Humes, lawyer and author, former White House speech writer and State Department planner. After all, the résumé sent to the program chairman is the only information the audience has on me. They want to believe I'm important or else they have wasted their evening coming to hear me.

Now there are some tips on how to seem more of an expert lecturer when speaking to your lodge on amateur photography or to your civic club on your recent trip to Moscow. But first let's treat the "easier" situation, in which you're the guest expert in the strange town.

I put the quotation marks around "easier" because, while it is easier to have yourself built up ten feet tall, you also have longer to fall if you are a disappointment. After all, you can't disappoint friends at Elks and Kiwanis too much; they didn't think you an expert in the first place—only a nice guy who happened to have an interesting experience or fascinating hobby.

First, the most important research you can do for your speech is not in the library but on the telephone to the program chairman. How big is the audience? Who is in it—professional people, businessmen, housewives, or mixed? What is the average

age? Are they college educated? Is he, the program chairman, going to send a release and your picture to the paper, or is there a publicity chairman? Is he, the program chairman, going to make the introduction or is someone else? To whom should you send biographical material?

When you send your biographical material, don't just send a copy of your latest job résumé. You are looking for a better introduction not better employment. Prepare another biographical background sheet. List all those activities that generally and specifically prepared you for your speech topic.

When I speak on a historical subject, I include the fact that I was a history major, that I have written numerous articles on history as well as two books, and that one of my interests is taking children to various historical sites around the country.

If I give a talk on crime, I emphasize that I'm a lawyer, a former state legislator and director of the Philadelphia Bar Association. In addition, I mention my experience as a state legislator and former staff member of the White House Policy Planning Section.

In other words, write down only data that would strengthen the thrust of an introduction. Does it really add anything when the introducer says that I was once chairman of Kiwanis Brotherhood Day or even that I have two daughters by the names of Mary and Rachel?

Instead, pick out from your education, travels, civic activities, hobbies, as well as job background, those items that add to your area of expertise. Then take that sheet of relevant data, put it into the envelope along with a glossy picture and a news release if you have one, and send it to the program chairman.

Of course, even then you still can't be sure of a good introduction. For that, there is only one sure-fire method—write your own. Do what George Bernard Shaw used to do in his early career. He wrote interviews of himself and submitted them to the paper. Write your own introduction. After years of speaking on an average of over once a week all over the country, I have learned through painful and embarrassing experiences how to write my own introduction and include it in my background material. Usually I append a note: "Enclosed is a copy of an introduction that was used recently. You might find it helpful."

> Our speaker today, James C. Humes, is a "Philadelphia lawyer," but like his eighteenth-century predecessors who helped forge the Declaration and the Constitution he is more than just a lawyer—he is a man of renaissance roles, many-sided in scope. He is also a lecturer, author, columnist, and TV performer. He has served in the State House as a legislator, in the White House as a speech writer, in the State Department as diplomat and planner. But, whether he is arguing in court as a public defender, debating in legislative halls, writing speeches for Presidents, lecturing in colleges, preaching from the pulpit, or acting on stage, one theme united all these strands of activities—love of words, both speaking and writing. Love of language is an attribute he shares with his boyhood hero Winston Churchill, whom he met while a schoolboy in England. In fact, he has two books on the subject—*Instant Eloquence* and *Podium Humor.* And "Instant Eloquence" is the subject of his speech tonight. . . .

Of course, the self-made introduction like the self-made man has its risks. Remember what the Illinois Congressman told Horace Greeley one day: "Mr. Greeley, you are looking at a self-made man." "That, sir," said Greeley, "relieves the Almighty of a great responsibility."

Pomposity is not an endearing trait in speakers. And yet how do you convey to the audience your background and accomplishments without appearing self-satisfied? The answer is— make an introducer tout your laurels and then you poke fun at yourself.

My brother Sam, who has a doctorate in government, tells of overhearing his son answering the phone and saying, "Yes, this is where Dr. Humes lives, but he's not the kind of doctor that does anybody any good."

In my opening remarks I sometimes tell about an incident shortly after I was appointed a White House Assistant. I flew home to Williamsport, the town of my birth, and struck up a conversation with an old baggage clerk while waiting to be picked up by a car. The old man didn't recognize me and thought I was a stranger to north central Pennsylvania. Along in the conversation I said, "Didn't I read somewhere that a guy from here is now working in the White House?" "Yup" was the reply. "Well, what do people say about that?" "They don't say anything—they just laugh."

The favorite ploy of Senators and Congressmen out on the hustings is the "negative name drop." The appeal of this gambit is that you can mention your fame and make fun of yourself all in the same breath. You tell of that embarrassing experience you had in the White House tripping Mrs. Ford, or how in Peking, halfway through the state dinner, a waiter brought you a knife and fork.

You see, the audience want to think you're famous but they don't want you to act as if you know it. So you tell them that you eat at the White House and visit China in ways that poke fun at yourself.

Women somehow seem to be more clever in picking up the negative name-drop technique ("There I was at the garden party at Buckingham Palace—the only person in a short dress." "I saw Leonard Bernstein at the exhibition and he said 'Dear, you must have gained ten pounds.' ") Any of us with some effort can go over some of our experiences with the high and the mighty and see what comical aspects there were to the meeting.

The appeal of the "famous and funny" ingredients to the lecture circuit illustrates another secret of speaking success. People want to be entertained as they are being enlightened. They want to laugh as they learn. A Ph.D. may enhance the credentials of the lecturer, but heaven help the lecturer who gives a speech on the doctoral dissertation that gave him the Ph.D.

Recently I talked on the phone to a woman who was program chairman of a luncheon meeting which I was to address. "Mr. Humes, we hear you are very entertaining. We like that—but don't think we'd be satisfied with just a succession of funny stories. That's like eating bonbons—it's fun while you eat them but afterward you feel guilty wondering why you did what you did. We want some meat with our dessert—we want to walk away from the speech with the feeling we got something solid to think about."

Perhaps the most successful American lecturer of all time was Mark Twain. Once at the end of a speech someone in the audience said, "Mr. Twain, you're amazing. You seem to know an anecdote to fit each point." Afterward, Twain confided to a friend, "What they don't know is that before each speech I run through all my stories and see which I can weave into my talk."

Look at this book. It's a lecture in written form. I use anecdotes like raisins in toast. It makes every bite, like every point, sweeter to swallow. That doesn't mean you have to buy a collection of humorous stories (although my book *Podium Humor* is, in my biased opinion, the best humor book for illustrating speech points). It does mean that you should ransack your memory for all comical personal experiences, funny stories, confrontations with the great, or anecdotes about famous people for a point or punch line that can dramatize a step in a how-to-do-it talk or an insight into a certain era of history.

If anecdotes and personal illustrations brighten a lecture, nothing deadens it so much as legalese, medicalese, bureaucratese or any other form of polysyllabic gobbledegook. When I was a teenager attending an English school, I was assigned a paper on eighteenth-century British poets. The due date arrived but my paper was not even begun. I called the house matron and told her to tell the infirmary that I was suffering from ergasiophobia and would have to stay in bed for the day. The distraught woman asked me what the symptoms were. I replied, "Fatigue and lack of energy." It took to the end of the day, when I had finished the paper, for the school doctor to find me out. "Humes," he said, "you do have 'ergasiophobia'—it means morbid aversion to work or just plain laziness."

Such an "inflated euphemism," in George Orwell's words, is verbal adolescence. It is how dull hacks, clerks, and drones talk when trying to look important.

On a television panel show I was once asked, "Mr. Humes, in

one word how would you explain your job as a White House speech writer?" I replied, "Translator—translating 'bureaucratese' into everyday language." If President Nixon was to give a speech on defense policy, I would rewrite a draft from the Pentagon. And, when a White House message on education was to be issued, there would be a draft from the Department of HEW. I had the job of translating "the viability of our defenses demands an optimal reliability of our systems' capabilities" or "participants will explore the concepts of communication, expressive arts, and the place of language skills in the developmental stages of the total person."

Winston Churchill's son Randolph once told me the reason for his father's success in oratory: "Father would translate latinate into Anglo-Saxon, 'perspiration' into 'sweat,' 'implements' into 'tools.' "

So as a lecturer be sure to translate all technical jargon into everyday English. With jargon you don't invite your listeners' enthusiasm or understanding of your field or hobby—be it aeronautics or numismatics, you only put them to sleep.

The great advantage of the "lecture" over the "advocacy" speech is that you don't have to do research in an unfamiliar field. You already know the subject. All you have to do is assemble the pieces of your knowledge in the right way. It is just a matter of organizing your facts and insights in the best framework.

That framework is *generalize—fragmentize—philosophize.* Imagine yourself on an afternoon helicopter tour of New York City. First at a distance you see the whole city spreading before you, then you pass over each of the sections and mark the special landmarks—the Statue of Liberty in the harbor; the Empire State Building, Rockefeller Center, the UN building, and Wall Street in Manhattan; Shea Stadium in Queens—and finally at dusk you fly away, seeing the profiled skyline. Or, to put it another way, you make your audience stand behind your shoulder—first at a distance to see the whole picture, then up close, and finally at a distance again as you sum up your impressions.

The artist Picasso once said the way to look at a painting is "to hang it a little crooked and stand back. Then you can get an arresting perspective."

How do you get the audience in the beginning to stand behind your shoulder. Well, for one thing you should try to explain the whole picture in terms of the audience's experience. For example, in 1963, I went to England on a lecture tour, speaking on our federalist system of government:

> Ladies and Gentlemen:
>
> Federalism, to you, is an abstraction about government—an equal relationship between the Federal Government in Washington and the various state capitols—how could that work? To you having local government in Buckinghamshire or Yorkshire equal to Westminster is impossible? But actually you have a type of Federalism in Britain —you know—Northern Ireland has its own parliament like our individual states have their own legislature—it enacts its own domestic legislation—and it is as difficult for Westminster to send troops to Belfast to stop Catholic discrimination as it is for Washington to send troops to Jackson, Mississippi, to prevent discrimination against Negroes.

The opening "generalization" can be like a preface to a book or it may be a catchy description—something that gives the audience an overall view of the whole subject.

When I came back from a junior year abroad at the University of Madrid, I began speeches on the subject of Spain this way:

> Modern Europe stops at the Pyrenees. There, south of the French border, stands Medieval Europe—with the idealized gallantry of knights in Court and the naked brutality of "inquisition" arrest and torture. When you see a bullfight, it's like seeing a knight's joust— the outward forms of style and grace of clothes as animal brutality.

My English friend Jamie Dugdale gives many talks on art in this country to men's groups and business clubs. To get their attention he opens:

> Going to an art auction is like going to the stock market. There are the reliable blue-chip paintings of old masters, the paintings of faddish artists like the glamour stocks, and there are the unknowns with

long-term potential. Buying paintings is not only a less complex field
to master than the stock market, it is also less risky and a safer
investment.

Recently, I have been traveling the country speaking on the
subject "How to Cross the Potomac Without Drowning." Here
is the way I start:

> Washington is not like any other capital of the world. Unlike Lon-
> don, Paris, or Rome it has no first-rate orchestra or first-run theater.
> No—it is a company town just like Detroit is Motor City or Grand
> Rapids is Furniture City—but in this case, Washington, they put out
> not sedans or sofas but bills, regulations, executive orders. If you see
> people talking on a Detroit bus, it may be about a new-model car
> they have just recalled because of a bug in the transmission, but in
> Washington people on a bus would be talking about the new civil
> service bill the President has just vetoed. In short, Washington is a
> company town and the company is government.

After you provide an opening insight into your topic, you are
then ready for the main meat of the speech. Here is where you
"fragmentize." You know why I cut up the meat for my daughters at dinner? Not because they could not do it themselves but
because the big slab of beef does not look appetizing—it is too
much to tackle. But, once I carve it up in small pieces, they start
on the meat and end up eating it all.

In how-to-do-it speeches on photography or furniture refin-
ishing, you break your speech up into five or six easy steps. In
a speech on the stock market you may divide it up into stocks,
bonds, and mutual funds. A book reviewer may talk on the plot,
characterizations, and style. You may separate a historical address into time periods or a travelogue into geographical re-
gions.

When I deliver my "Crossing the Potomac" speech, I tell the
audience that Washington like Gaul is divided into three parts
—Bureaucratic Washington, Diplomatic Washington, and Political Washington.

And in giving my speech entitled "Instant Eloquence," I
divide it into the E.A.S.E. acronym of advocacy speeches, *exem-*

plify, amplify, specify, electrify.
The U.S. artist Robert Henri once gave some advice about painting that could be applied to "lecture fragmentizing." "Every stave in a picket fence should be drawn with wit, the wit of one who sees each stave as new evidence about the fence. The staves should not repeat each other. A new fence is stiff but it doesn't stand long before there is movement through it, which is the trace of its life experience." And so with wit, insight, and imagination you should describe each era of the Aztec civilization, each step in cooking a soufflé, or each city in your trip to the Orient. A lecturer is a historian, guide, or explorer but above all he is a teacher. And, as Anatole France said, "The art of teaching is the art of making an audience so curious that they would like one day to try it themselves."

Any lecture should be a story of adventure—exploring the kitchen, risking an investment, discovering antiques, trekking through Africa, fathoming the intrigues of *Realpolitik,* examining prehistoric fossils, snaring the inside tidbits of Hollywood gossip, mastering the tricks of copywriting or the techniques of Georgetown party giving.

During the Middle Ages three stonemasons were asked what they were doing as they were working on their jobs. One looked down and said, "I am shaping stone." And the second said as he looked up, "I am making a wall." But the third proudly proclaimed, "I am building a cathedral."

What a philosophy to live by—not only in work but in our interests! And we should communicate the insights that we have learned from our vocation and avocation. That is the final part of the lecture—"philosophize." "Philosophy," wrote Rabelais, "is nothing but sophisticated poetry to sum things up." And that is what you do in your closing of a lecture. You sum up your impressions or insights.

When I closed my speech about Washington life, I said:

We make so much fun of politicians, it is a wonder that enough people are willing to risk their careers to enter public life. Politicians, you know, rank in a recent national poll on occupations nine-teenth—just above used-car dealers. What an irony—the American dream is that every child can grow up to be President, but a Gallup poll says 86 per cent of the mothers interviewed don't want their child to go into politics.

Yet I believe our bureaucratic system is as Churchill said, the worst form of government except for every other that has been tried from time to time. Sure, our country has not lived up to its ideals, but then no country ever had higher ideals to live up to.

I ended my Spanish talk with these words:

I remember a short story once about a Spanish prison—two prison-ers, a pale-faced aristocratic soldier and a swarthy peasant thief played checkers with religious relics on the squares made by the shadows projected from a gridiron window. And this black-and-white picture said much about life in Spain—where pure idealism lives side by side with dark earthiness—where each Spaniard can pray like an El Greco saint and play like a Goya sinner—where each Spaniard is both a Don Quixote and a Sancho Panza.

With such a close a reader may say, "That's fine for the profes-sional lecturer, but I would look a little foolish waxing so elo-quent on home photography to the boys from the Elks lodge." The answer is, say what you have learned in your heart about your job or hobby.

Don't worry about being a lecturer, even in your own home town. All you have to remember is three things. First, don't read your speech.

A young man giving a lecture for the first time asked Winston Churchill how he thought his speech went. Churchill replied, "First, you read your speech; second, you read it badly; and third, it wasn't worth reading."

If you are an expert, you don't read a speech. You choose a subject you know so well you can talk thirty minutes just refer-ring to notes.

And second, if you use visuals like slides don't let the machine master the man. No lecturer should play introducer to every picture or every rock. It is the quickest way to put your audience to sleep. Remember, you are not an "usher" but a "professor." Your visual should reinforce your message and not say it for you. Don't let flip cards be the speech. Only use a picture when it is worth a thousand words.

Third, try to talk slowly and even quietly. Sam Ervin once told me that only young men unsure of themselves—unsure that they can keep their audience's attention—speak loud and fast. It is the judge, the philosopher, or the professor who speaks slowly and quietly—knowing every word will be weighed as wisdom.

CHAPTER 4

The Speaker as Commemorator

> "You'll never move others, heart to heart, unless you
> speak from the heart."
>
> GOETHE

If the prototype for an advocate may be a lawyer, and the model for a lecturer may be a professor, who best exemplifies the commemorator? I think a minister. In my childhood in Williamsport, Pennsylvania, there was a Presbyterian pastor from Harrisburg who sometimes supplied our church in times of ministerial vacancy. His name was Dr. C. Walter Cherry.

I am sure almost everyone remembers from their youth a certain minister, priest, or rabbi who seemed to radiate wisdom and strength. Dr. Cherry was that type of minister. He was the first minister whose sermons I remember actually listening to. Yet, though he was able to reach the mind and heart of a nine-year-old, he was a Biblical scholar of no little erudition. He was both pure in heart and bright in mind. He had a smile that was benign on a head that was almost leonine. But what I remember most was the settling presence when he entered a room or mounted a pulpit. It was a peace that brought understanding. Whether he was giving an invocation at a dinner, greeting visitors to the church, or consoling a young boy like myself who had just lost his father, his words and voice always struck the right note. He could establish a mood of thanksgiving, a sense of welcome, or a feeling of compassion.

Such is the role of the commemorator. He doesn't exhort like the advocate or explain like the lecturer—he establishes a mood or expresses a feeling. Perhaps it is joy and hope at the time of a cornerstone dedication, or regret and good wishes at a retirement ceremony, or lament and consolation in a eulogy.

The commemorator doesn't so much want his audience to act or to understand as he wants them to feel—to feel hope, thanksgiving, or renewed dedication. In Webster's Third International Dictionary the first definition of "commemorate" is: "to call to remembrance (as by speech, writing, or ceremony)."

Speakers often slight the importance of the commemorative speech. They regard it as a trite exercise—something like mouthing the words of the Pledge of Allegiance or "The Star-Spangled Banner." It is something to be gotten over with. To many speakers, the commemorative speech does not rank very high in priority—after all, it is not as noble as the lecture, which teaches, or the advocacy speech, which reforms.

Of course, such an attitude misses the point that two of the greatest speeches of all time were commemorative—the Gettysburg Address and Pericles' Funeral Oration to the Athenians. In my own career of more than a thousand speeches or talks, the two that moved the audience the most and are best remembered were a eulogy of John Kennedy in the Pennsylvania House of Representatives and a memorial address in honor of Sir Winston Churchill. Why are the commemorative speeches better remembered than advocacy talks or "lectures"?

Well, for one thing, a commemorative speech is a ceremony or a rite. We remember the time they presented a gold watch to Joe for thirty years' service long after a travelogue on Norway is forgotten. We remember the day they dedicated the hospital wing long after some speech arguing against the Bricker Amendment. The hot issue of ten or even five years ago has burned out and the cold ashes scattered. Yet certain ceremonies illuminate the past and bring dimension to our memories— "That was the year Bill was installed as Rotary president" or "It was just about this time last year the company had the retirement dinner for Bob." There is another good reason audiences are likely to remember commemorative occasions more than speeches or lectures. That is because feelings have more impact than facts.

The problem, though, with many commemorators is that they do nothing to arouse feelings. By just going through the motions, they don't stir the emotions.

My cousin Ambassador John Humes was one of the most popular envoys ever assigned to Vienna. One of the reasons Austria loved him was the way he represented the United States at all those ceremonies, dedications, and luncheons that where an ambassador must appear and say a few words. It was not that the speeches were remembered as particularly eloquent, witty, or profound but rather that he is remembered as being sincere, warm, and *gemütlich*. Each audience he addressed came away thinking their occasion was something special. How did he do it? He did it by talking about his feelings. You don't have to be an orator to be able to express feelings. You just have to be sincere. You have to think beforehand what a man or an institution has meant to you and say it.

A good way to sort out your feelings is to recall an incident or experience that epitomizes your thoughts. After all, to "commemorate" means to call to remembrance—nothing more sentimental than some nostalgic note of the past. Thomas Wolfe may have written *You Can't Go Home Again* but we sure do try —to relive those days when everything seemed clearer and simpler. What else explains the nostalgic crazes for the films of the forties or songs of the fifties? E. M. Forster wrote: "In the heart of each there is contrived, by desperate devices, a magical island. . . . We place it in the past for safety. . . . We call it memory, but it is not—it is the outcome of our anxiety with the world we have made."

The Spanish have a word for this hunger for yesterday—it is *saudade*. García Lorca, the Spanish poet uses it when he writes, "If only I could recapture the dreams of yesterday."

So the first rule for a commemorative speech is to evoke a memory. That's easy to keep in mind because the word "commemorate" has the core of memory within it. When you have to deliver a commemorative address—whether it be some short remarks on Veterans Day or when pinning on an Eagle Scout badge—think of some incident. Perhaps it was a battlefield situation in World War II or Korea, or maybe it was something your old scoutmaster taught you as a boy. Retell the experience and then the impressions it made and the lessons it taught. A commemorative speech should be impressionistic.

In a way, speeches are like paintings. The bold lines of a modern abstraction are like those of an advocacy speech—the simplistic and dramatic presentation of an idea. The lecture on the other hand, is more like illustrative realism—perhaps the detailed picture by a Wyeth telling you something about a field or a farm girl. But the commemorative speech is more like an impressionist painting—a picture with warm colors and texture capturing a mood or a moment.

One of my favorite mystery writers, Ross MacDonald, has one of his characters say, "The painter makes objects out of events, the poet makes words out of events." Or, to put it another way, the commemorator paints for the audience a word picture of a certain memory or event he experienced. He gets the audience to share with him the impressions of that memory.

Surely you have heard Bob Hope's signature song, "Thanks for the Memory." In the song the theme line "Thanks for the memory" is always followed by two or three things—"of candlelight and wine and castles on the Rhine" or "of gardens at Versailles and beef and kidney pie." In a sense this is how you prepare for a few words in a commemorative talk. You think of a poignant experience in the life of a man or an institution and then talk about three aspects of the man or institution that the incident revealed.

Some years ago I was asked to present to Lord Avon (formerly Sir Anthony Eden), a key to the town of Edenton, North Carolina, a town named after the ex-prime minister's ancestor Sir Charles Eden, the first Governor of North Carolina. In making the presentation at Avon's home I spoke of the young Eden, the dashing cabinet officer who risked his whole career by resigning from the Chamberlain government in opposition to policies he characterized as appeasement to Hitler. Here was a young man at the pinnacle of power giving it all up on a matter of conscience.

And then I dwelt on three qualities the incident revealed; his devotion to freedom, his love of country, and his loyalty to principle. Each quality was expanded into a paragraph.

When I was at the White House, I was invited to speak to the Hill School in Pottstown, Pennsylvania, which I had attended as a boy. I talked of the last speech my father had ever prepared —a speech on a revered teacher, Alfred Rolfe, who had been a master during three generations of my family. The speech was never given because my father had a seizure on the way to the speech and died. I went on to give the essence of that speech which had never before been delivered—that Alfred Rolfe had been a scholar, a gentleman, and a friend who taught by his example. I went on to say how those qualities, scholarship, honor, and friendship, were the values we as students came to appreciate in our years at school.

Again, you have the commemorator technique—recreate the memorable scene and then draw two or three lessons from the scene. In my book *Instant Eloquence* I talked about this method in my discussion of "Soul-Shakers." "Soul-Shakers," I said, were those poignant vignettes out of history which could be used as a dramatic endings to advocacy speeches or as catchy beginnings to ceremonial remarks.

The effectiveness of such "soul-shaking" stories is this: you borrow on the poignancy of some emotion-filled occasion out of history and use it to uplift your own remarks. In the case of an advocacy speech there may be nothing intrinsically eloquent in asking the city council for a new rent-control act. But you can give an electrifying close with this story:

> In the days of Periclean Greece, where democracy all began, a great philosopher was once approached by a citizen with this question: "Sir, when will justice come to Athens?" And Thucydides replied,

"Justice will not come to Athens until those who are not exploited are as indignant as those who are exploited."

Sometimes in ceremonial remarks you cannot think of an incident of memorable impact. So you adopt one out of history. In 1971, I was asked to represent President Nixon in throwing out the ball for the Little League World Series in Williamsport, Pennsylvania. Now, though I grew up and played baseball in this town where Little League baseball all started, I could not think of any poignant memory in my own background that would launch a few remarks. So I began this way:

> In 1945 Branch Rickey stunned the sporting world by announcing he was going to hire the Negro baseball star Jackie Robinson. A fellow club owner reprimanded the Brooklyn Dodger president, saying, "Branch, you're rocking the boat—why are you opening up this controversial subject?" And Rickey replied, "Because I want to make major league baseball an All-American game."
>
> And similarly I am proud my home town of Williamsport has made Little League baseball an all-world game—a sport now played in thirty-two countries.

I then went on to talk about the contributions Little League made in developing young bodies and nurturing values of sportsmanship and fair play.

Actually, it was my vast collection of "soul-shaker" stories that led to my appointment to the White House staff as a speech writer. Nixon as Vice President came to know of my story file when I was doing some part-time work for him while going through law school in Washington. So, when he was elected President, he asked me to come down and try my hand at drafting some of the presidential remarks. Most of my work at the White House consisted of writing lines for the so-called "Rose Garden rubbish"—that is the ceremonial remarks the President often makes in the Rose Garden. It could be welcoming astronauts, honoring national officers of the Girl Scouts, or introducing a new cabinet official after the swearing-in. In other words, these were commemorative-type speeches such as each of us might have to make one time or another—welcoming a foreign dignitary with a key to city hall, honoring the safety-award winner, or introducing the new president of the Rotary.

When I speak around the country on my White House experience, members of the audience often ask me, "Why does a President have to have a speech writer? Surely in the case of these simple ceremonial remarks, the President could think of something to say on his own." The answer is that anything the President says, even in informal remarks, is part of the public record. So it behooves the President to say something more than "How are you—you're doing a great job!" To do that, though, means doing some background research on Astronaut Borman or the Girl Scouts. That takes time and that is what the President does not have. So the speech writer is asked to come up with a draft for the occasion.

Even for a five- or ten-minute speech it is not that easy. In fact, it is, in a way, tougher for the White House writer than preparing a major foreign-policy address. At least in the latter case one has before him a draft sent over by the State Department or National Security Council. You only have to translate the draft into powerful rhetoric. But, in the instance of a Rose Garden welcome speech, one has to think of something original about an occasion that has been performed a hundred times before. It is like being an editorial writer for a newspaper—having to write something new and untrite for the column space on Thanksgiving or Lincoln's Birthday.

When Woodrow Wilson was Governor of New Jersey, he once accepted an invitation to give an hour address some five weeks thence. Later, the program chairman called and explained that there were some complications. Could he instead stop over the next week and deliver some five minutes of informal remarks? Wilson said no—that it wasn't enough of an advance warning. "What do you mean?" said the chairman. "You'll only have to speak for five minutes." "Yes," said Wilson, "but it is those short speeches that require the most preparation." Wilson knew that Lincoln did not give the seven-minute Gettysburg Address off the cuff. He spent more than seven days preparing for it. Well, you won't have to spend seven days preparing for your short remarks in the Memorial Day program, but you are going to have to think about it beforehand. You are going to have to ransack your memory for that personal incident or that vignette out of history.

I recall in 1969 when I was asked to represent the President at the Fourth of July ceremonies at Independence Hall. I opened this way:

> Over a hundred years ago at similar ceremonies at Faneuil Hall on the Fourth of July Rufus Choate gave the featured address. When he was finished, E. J. Dickinson turned to him on the speaker's dais and said, "You certainly rang out all the glittering generalities." And Ralph Waldo Emerson responded: "No! Words about the Declaration of Independence are not glittering generalities but blazing ubiquities—meaningful for all countries and all ages."
>
> Today I would like to address myself briefly to three of those truths that our forefathers found self-evident: the right to life, or security of the individual and his home; the right to liberty, or the freedom to speak and worship as you please; and the pursuit of happiness, or the chance to seek your own endeavor or opportunity.

With a little research you can come up with something new and profound. My friend Donald W. Whitehead, Federal Co-Chairman of the U.S. Appalachian Regional Commission, last year was asked to give a Memorial Day address in upstate Pennsylvania. His opener was this paragraph:

> All of us think we know those immortal words of the Declaration of Independence, "We hold these truths to be self-evident that all men are created equal—that they are endowed by their creator with certain . . ." What is the next word?—Is it "inalienable" or "unalienable" rights? Well, in a sense, both are right. Thomas Jefferson wrote in his draft "inalienable" rights but the Committee of Revision, consisting of Ben Franklin and John Adams, must have changed it because the official document—the one kept in the National Archives—reads "unalienable rights." Now why did the committee change the word—does it make any difference? "Inalienable" is a current legal word describing rights that cannot involuntarily be

taken away but you can voluntarily sell them or deed them away. On the other hand, "unalienable" is an archaic, eighteenth-century word describing rights given by God in trust which you cannot give away. Indeed, you have a duty to your children and children's children to preserve and guard them.

At this point the reader might complain and say, "I don't have time to spend hours in the library searching out the right historical incident. How can I find the right commemorative speech opener when no incident in my own personal experience comes to mind?"

Raymond Chandler once advised writers of detective stories, "When you're stuck for an opening have a man come through the door with a gun." Well, I will offer you not one door but five doors, or to be more precise—five possible approaches.

In my book *Podium Humor* I offered the acronym P.I.T.C.H. —so called because the speech writers for Eisenhower in the 1956 whistle-stop campaign would ask what the pitch was on Johnstown, say—meaning what is its history, its industry, its famous features, and favorite sons.

P.I.T.C.H. stands for *purpose* of the occasion; the *institution* so honored; the *time* of its inception or what it was like then; the *city* involved; and the *hero* or great man connected with the organization or movement.

Let's say you are asked to represent the local bar association and deliver some remarks on Law Day. Well, what is the purpose of the day? Originally it was established to counter the Soviet Government May Day celebration, in which they parade their tanks and armies down Red Square. Now, is there some experience where you as a lawyer have helped a client successfully appeal a government ruling? This could be a dramatic example of how in a democracy the individual armed with the rule of law can triumph against the might of the state. Or you can talk about how the Calley case represented the first time a country ever prosecuted its own soldiers for brutality in wartime. Or that

Watergate showed "that no man, not even the President, is above the law in America."

Secondly, you think of some actions your local bar association has taken in your city such as helping to set up a lawyers' ethics investigatory panel or a police review board. It is difficult to imagine a better example of the rule of law than a case where a possibly overzealous police action against a citizen was checked by a review board investigation.

Third, you might want to look back to the time the bar association was founded in your town. What have been the legal milestones taken in securing civil liberties of individuals since that time? Have you had any personal experience as a lawyer in which Supreme Court decisions on civil liberties would have affected the course of the trial?

Fourth, has your city been the site of any important legal decisions or the host of an important convention on human rights? Possibly you or your family have been involved in one of those decisions or played a role as delegates. Or maybe the city is famous as the home or birthplace of a famous lawyer or legislator. Not long ago, when I was giving commemorative remarks as a lawyer in Clarksburg, West Virginia, I discovered in my speech research that Clarksburg was the host to an important convention at the time of the Civil War which led to West Virginia's siding with the Union and against slavery. I also found out that the mountain town was the home of John W. Davis—the former Ambassador to England and the 1924 Democratic presidential candidate—whose legal brief in 1952 prevented President Harry Truman from illegal seizure of the steel mills.

And lastly is some "hero" or legal giant whose life can give you a story by which to begin your Law Day remarks:

Learned Hand, one of the greatest appellate judges, once got into a legal argument with Oliver Wendell Holmes. "But," remonstrated

Hand, "we have a court of justice." "No," corrected the Justice. "We have a court of law." Holmes went on to explain that "laws" were not the ideal of freedom but rather the means or tools by which we try to achieve the ideal of justice.

Or perhaps you could use something like the following to open your remarks:

> During some congressional investigations of land sales before World War I, Boston lawyer Louis Brandeis appeared before the committee as a representative of a group of citizens alarmed at the waste. When he took the witness stand, a Congressman challenged his right to be present.
>
> "Who, sir," he asked, "do you represent? Who is the client retaining you?"
>
> "I, sir," replied the future Supreme Court Justice, "represent the people. The public is my client."

Of all commemorative speeches the ones most difficult to prepare are often the eulogies. If you ever have tried to write a condolence letter, you know how painful the task can be. Yet, if you concentrate on how you came to know the deceased or on some intimate glimpse of a side of his character, the rest of the remarks will flow quite naturally. As you "commemorate" him, think of that memorable accomplishment or magnanimous deed that so expressed his consideration of others or his love of people.

Sometimes, of course, you did not know the deceased personally. In this case you may have to borrow from history or literature for the story to strike just the right chord of remembrance and sympathy. I have heard eulogists, for example, quote Shakespeare,

> His life was gentle, and the elements
> So mix'd in him that Nature might stand up
> And say to all the world, "This was a man!"

In 1969 as Executive Director of the Philadelphia Bar Association, I was asked to deliver a few brief remarks for a memorial

service for the slain Martin Luther King. At that time I quoted
Auden's words about Yeats:

> . . . May I
> Beleaguered by the same
> Negation and despair
> Show an affirming flame.

CHAPTER 5

The Speaker as Toastmaker

> "His words are a very fantastical banquet."
> SHAKESPEARE, *Much Ado About Nothing*

Do you know someone who has been best man at a score of weddings and a godfather for a slew of children? It seems as if he is on the board of every school he ever attended, and every club of which he is a member. It is not that he seeks such honors or burdens but rather that he is the one everyone turns to—whether for advice or sympathy. He may not be an actual uncle but "avuncular" fits his description—always remembering with a graduation gift or birthday card. And there is one other thing friends and family always expect of him—to rise and say the appropriate words for a toast.

I have a distant cousin like that. He can be counted on to give a toast at any wedding or other family occasion. He gives such toasts warmly and gracefully. Why does he do so? Is it because he likes to tell stories and be center stage? No—it is because he is a gentleman who thinks that a toast is sometimes called for —just like a thank-you note or a condolence letter.

And my cousin makes a good toast because he always has something to say. He doesn't just wish the bride happiness or the bridegroom congratulations. He recounts some incident—the time his niece brought home a stray puppy or the time his godson sent him the belt he made as a Cub Scout. He tells such stories lovingly and sees in them the qualities that would make a marriage strong.

A good toast may be warm and witty but it should have some

substance. Too often it is a cliché as empty as a champagne bubble or as flat as yesterday's wine. Actually, the very origin of the toast suggests that there be something substantive. The Vikings put pieces of bread toasted by the fire into their wooden wine chalices. The word "toast" comes from that tradition. Similarly, you should put something solid into your message.

Sir Winston Churchill once said of a colleague in the House of Commons: "He is one of those who before they get up, do not know what they are going to say; when they are speaking, do not know what they are saying; and when they have sat down, do not know what they have said."

There is only one rule for a successful toast: know what you are going to say. Think of that incident or experience that offers a personal glimpse or insight into the person you are toasting. More than once I have composed my wedding-reception toast during the marriage ceremony. Even if I looked strangely preoccupied, it didn't matter. All eyes were on the bride anyway.

How many times have we seen someone rise to give a toast whose only preparation has been liquid? What the porter in *Macbeth* said about sex and drinking can apply to a toast: "It provokes and unprovokes: it provokes the desire, but it takes away the performance." A few more glasses of wine may give you the will to rise but not the words to speak. Not that I'm against wine. Far from it. As a matter of fact, I agree with what Alben Barkley once told Adlai Stevenson: "The best audience is one that is intelligent, well-educated, and a little drunk." A gathering where champagne has flowed freely is a responsive audience. They will applaud almost anything. They will laugh at almost every line if you give them half a chance. All you have to do is mention some idiosyncrasy of a person everyone knows about or some escapade everyone has heard about. I have been at anniversary receptions where an eighty-year-old great-grandmother was wildly applauded and at weddings where the young kid brother got a tremendous hand.

In 1959 when my brother Sam was married to a Dutch girl

in The Hague, I gave a toast I had memorized in Dutch. I was the hit of the wedding reception. But then I had to tell some of the Netherlanders that it was not that difficult because after all I had studied German for three years. The Dutch maintain with considerable academic authority that Dutch is closer to English than German, the language of their past enemy. It just goes to show you, you should not be too eager to explain your technique or success. It rarely adds to your effort.

Any toast, as long as it is not the rambling, incoherent, drunken variety, will be a welcome addition to the festivities. Like the awkward birthday gift, it is the thought behind it that counts. At one golden anniversary I heard one toaster read Edgar Guest's "It takes a heap of livin' . . . t' make it home." And at a wedding I attended a father offered the simple if unoriginal note, "I have not lost a daughter—I have gained a son." Both, since sincerely given, were sincerely appreciated.

Speaking of poetry, even the most doggerel kind is not out of place at a family affair. Just remember one rule: Don't read it from a piece of paper—unless it is your own. Then be sure to write it out so the recipient can keep it as a memento of the occasion. I remember once I composed a fifty-verse poem on the occasion of a birthday party for my cousin John Humes at the embassy in Vienna. Though it does not read so well now, it provided much fun at the time of the rendition. Rhyming verse is not hard. If you have the biographical details, it is only a matter of sitting down and doing it. I remember writing my "masterpiece" while traveling on the airplane.

In fact, the secret of any toast is taking the time beforehand to organize your thoughts. Let me give two examples of toasts at weddings where I was an usher. As I rummaged through my memory, I came up with these incidents. In the first, I recalled that the romance began in camp when the couple stayed up all night in a rowboat to see the sunrise. In the second wedding, I remembered that my friendship began with the bridegroom when we, along with another six-year-old, were angels in the church pageant. So I worked my toasts this way:

It is said that a shipboard romance should give caution—that a wedding where the two met and fell in love on an ocean liner does not have the solidest prospects. So I think as an usher it is incumbent on me to warn that the relationship of this marriage began in a boat romance. I was there that night when it sailed but it wasn't from a pier in New York but a dock in camp. In fact, it wasn't a ship but a rowboat. The music they listened to wasn't the shipboard orchestra but the rhythmic squeaking of the wooden craft. And their feet were not waltzing through the air but soaking in sloshy pools of hull-filled water. And what they had to drink were not bottles of cold light champagne but cans of warm dark root beer. And yet despite such romantic trappings they stayed up to see the dawn—the first day of their new relationship.

So today I want to toast the first day in another stage of that relationship. May their rowboat sail smoothly.

As I witnessed the beautiful wedding ceremony today in this church, I couldn't help but reflect that the friendship of the bridegroom and myself began in church—unlikely as that may seem. He and I along with another pal were the haloed angels in the Christmas church pageant. But the minister unfortunately thought the three of us, with our many pranks, would have been better fitted for playing in *Faust*. In fact the minister called us the unholy trio. But oh what advances the groom has made since the time in that church to this one—now we can all see he has found a real angel—and he has been promoted from the depths of being called one of an "unholy trio" to the heights of being called one of a "blessed duo." To the blessed duo.

Now I present these wedding toasts not to prove my creative ability but rather to prove that any toast that is well thought out will be well received. In fact, if my memory doesn't fail me, they were thought to be uproariously funny. Why? It certainly doesn't read that way. Well, half of the secret is a merry audience, but the other half is the technique of giving the toast.

Once Art Buchwald gave these two tips on writing humor. The first, the narrator should play it straight. Secondly, he should treat the serious as light and the light as serious. The same holds true for giving a toast. Play it deadpan—don't laugh or even grin at your own talking—no matter how much they laugh. And, second, mix into your philosophy a measure of humor.

Scotty Smith, the daughter of F. Scott Fitzgerald, once told me of her father's advice to her, "A great social success is a pretty girl who plays her cards as if she were plain." And, similarly, a successful toaster is one who plays funny lines as if they were straight.

Last year at the end of a graduation ceremony a father rose to say a few words. "My daughter asked me not to talk too long, not to talk about her, and not to talk about the way things were when I was her age. So, in conclusion . . ." said President Gerry Ford with a straight face.

Some of the best toasts I have ever heard at weddings have come from literature. At one wedding of a gorgeous bride to a friend of mine, the best man said, "Somerset Maugham once wrote that American women expect to find in their husbands a perfection that English women only hope to find in their butlers. In that case there may be some disappointment. But I will say this—that in this bride there is the perfection French men would only expect from their mistresses."

At another wedding reception the Episcopal rector gave this toast:

> When I first met this beautiful bride-to-be it was at my study in the manse. When I escorted her to the door, I tripped. My thoughts then, as they are today, keep turning back to that description in Raymond Chandler's mystery book *Farewell, My Lovely:* "She was a blonde—a blonde beautiful enough to make a bishop kick a hole in a stained-glass window." Well, I have not heard of any breakage at the cathedral but I'll tell you one thing, she is beautiful enough to make a vicar fall on his face.

At a wedding of a friend to a beautifully built Southern belle, I toasted this way:

> Marriage, it is said, began with a wife reforming a husband. That may be needed but I would not like to see any alterations in the bride. It reminds me of Supreme Court Chief Justice Salmon Chase

at a reception during the Reconstruction Era who eyed a damsel with similar proportions of beauty as the bride today. The Justice tried to make the acquaintance of the young lady, whose hour-glass gown showed off her assets to great advantage. "Madam, I am Salmon Chase." "I know well who you are, Mr. Chief Justice, but I want to warn you I am still an unreconstructed rebel." "Madam," he replied gazing at her beautiful figure, "in your case reconstruction would be blasphemous." And so I propose a toast to a beautiful girl who needs no alterations.

Quotations from literature or history don't even have to be funny. At one wedding after a whirlwind courtship an usher quoted Marcel Proust: "Love is the space and time measured by the heart."

At another the uncle said of the bride:

When I think of her, I recall the exchange about charm in Sir James Barrie's play *What Every Woman Knows.* "What *is* charm exactly?" it is asked. "Oh," is the reply, "it's a sort of bloom on a woman. If you have it, you don't need to have anything else; and if you don't have it, it doesn't matter what else you have. Some women, the few, have charm for all; and most have charm for one. But some have charm for none." Well, our girl has charm and a lot more—like beauty, brains, and caring for others. But I would like to make a toast to one who has charm for all and charm for one.

Many of the stories I tell are about my favorite hero Sir Winston Churchill. At one anniversary I quoted Churchill's letter from the trenches in World War I to be opened if he died, "On the whole since I have met you, my darling one, I have been happy and you have taught me how noble a woman's heart can be."

But my all-time favorite Churchill story and toast for both weddings and anniversaries is this:

The beautiful qualities of the bride are too numerous to mention— her grace, her loveliness, her warmth, her smile, her loyalty, and her love—she will be both a shelter and a source of inspiration. And I am confident that the groom could one day say what Winston

Churchill said near the end of his life. It was at the Savoy Hotel in London at a banquet attended by most of the notables of Britain. It was a tradition at this particular banquet to put on some sort of public charade. The game that night was: "If you couldn't be who you are, who would you like to be?" Each of the dignitaries had to answer the question by rising and making a toast to some figure out of history. Of course, the audience was breathless with anticipation as to how Churchill would respond. After all, a Churchill wouldn't want to be a Julius Caesar or Napoleon. When Churchill, as ranking member of the occasion, rose as the last speaker, he said, "If I can't be who I am, I would most like to be"—and then the seventy-eight-year-old Sir Winston turned to touch his wife's hand—"Lady Churchill's second husband."

The formal toasts at the Savoy Hotel banquet Churchill attended remind me that there are really two kinds of toasts—the family and the formal. The family occasion is the wedding or anniversary party. But the formal one is where the toast is obligatory. In Britain, for example, at a black-tie dinner you cannot smoke until the monarch is toasted. Once General Eisenhower at a Guild Hall dinner in 1945 started to take out a cigarette. But fortunately Viscount Alexander spotted him and jumped up quickly and said, "The King," before Ike could light it. In Scotland you will note the practice of raising the wine glasses over the water goblets. The reason for such a tradition dates back to three hundred years ago when the dethroned Stuart dynasts were in exile in France. So, when Scottish loyalists had to rise and toast the British monarch, they were toasting the King "over the water"—meaning over the seas in France.

Well, it's all right to drink over the water glass as long as you don't toast *with* the water glass. Secretary of State William Jennings Bryan attended in 1914 the Japanese Embassy party celebrating the tenth anniversary of Japan's defeat of the Russian Navy. When the teetotaling Bryan began his toast with his water glass he could see that he had offended the Japanese. But he recovered saying, "Since the Imperial Japanese Navy won a great victory on water, I will toast in water; when they win on wine, I will then toast in wine." At formal receptions you should toast with wine and not with martinis or manhattans. And you don't signal your toast by beating your spoon on the plate or glass.

In the White House I used to draft some of the toasts for visiting heads of state. It was a chore I enjoyed since I usually then got an invitation to the dinner. Here, preliminary drafts of the toasts were outlined by the State Department. I remember one toast I wrote for a dinner honoring Canadian Prime Minister Pierre Trudeau. Through research I had found a line from Trudeau's doctoral thesis on Sir Wilfrid Laurier, the founder of the Canadian Liberal party: "He had the courage to swim upstream." But when I used this for the draft of the toast, I was bawled out by Henry Kissinger for being too generous to the Canadian Prime Minister.

At some state dinners there can be sensitive feelings. The Civil War almost started thirty years early when President Andrew Jackson by means of a toast tried to put his states-rights Vice President John C. Calhoun on the spot. "To the Constitution," Jackson said as he raised his glass, "may it long be preserved." But Calhoun responded, "To the Constitution, next to liberty most dear."

Of course, most presidential toasts are not that controversial. Their themes are about as original and inspiring as the two types of gifts that American Presidents always present to visiting heads of government—Steuben sculptured glass or Boehm porcelain birds. Similarly, Presidents always talk about the greatness of the Thai people or the bonds of friendship between France and the United States.

Some of our statesmen rise above the prosaic. Dean Acheson at a white-tie dinner in Paris once rose to contemplate aloud the names of the great luminaries who had graced this salon with their presence:

> The limping Prince of Benevento, Monsieur de Talleyrand, the handsome and wise English statesman Lord Castlereagh, the silent and watchful Viennese diplomat Metternich, the liberal talking au-

tocrat Czar Alexander I, the dour Prussian Chancellor von Bismarck, the urbane Britisher Benjamin Disraeli, the pragmatic Italian politician Cavour—If all of these, separated by geography or century, gathered in one room at one time what would they talk about? Well, I put that question to Oliver Wendell Holmes, to whom I was a law clerk, and he answered, "They would find a way to talk," he said, "through a series of interpreters and the talk would be about the one subject they would all have in common—the grace, charm and beauty of the women present."

A Frenchman, Ambassador Paul Claudel, in the depression-racked and war-threatening 1930s responded to the necessity of a toast this way at a reception in Washington, "Gentlemen, in the little moment that remains between the crisis and the catastrophe, we might as well take a glass of champagne."

At a reception honoring the twentieth anniversary of NATO in 1969 a Belgian diplomat toasted Harry S. Truman for his efforts in forging the European defense shield, "One of the greatest European diplomats, Prince Talleyrand, once wrote, 'The art of statesmanship is to foresee the inevitable and to expedite its occurrence.' I salute a great performer as well as prophet, Harry S. Truman."

At this point the reader may say, "Well, I don't go to embassy parties." No, but all of us at one time or another do attend formal dinners where we sometimes have to toast the host or honoree. At a New York theater party I attended, the leading lady toasted the leading man quoting Toots Shor's remark to Jimmy Walker: "Whenever you walked in, you brightened up the joint."

And at a political dinner I heard Governor Scranton of Pennsylvania toasted with the words of the cable Franklin Delano Roosevelt sent to Churchill on his birthday, "Winston, it is fun to be in the same decade with you."

At one recent Philadelphia dinner party I heard one of the guests pay this graceful tribute to the hostess. Borrowing a line attributed to Perle Mesta she said: "For many years I have tried to figure out the secret of her success as a party giver. It's more than just her beautiful home, her delicious food or her vintage wine—it's a matter of three words. When I arrive she always says to me, 'At last,' and when I am about to leave she always says, 'Already?' "

Even if we may not be called on to give toasts to foreign countries and their leaders at embassy parties, some of us do attend formal dinners of patriotic or ethnic organizations.

At a Colonial Society dinner in Philadelphia, I toasted our Founding Fathers this way:

> In the 1870s the Ambassador to the Court of St. James's was the poet and writer James Russell Lowell. One day the French historian Guizot, who was also the Ambassador to England, approached Lowell and asked, "Mr. Ambassador, how long will the American republic endure?" Lowell replied, "As long as the ideals of its leaders reflect the ideals of the Founding Fathers." To our Founding Fathers.

At a Friendly Sons of St. Patrick dinner in Philadelphia in 1972, I told the story of the abortive Risin' of 1798 when Irish patriots were slaughtered by the same Cornwallis who fought in the American Revolutionary War.

> The poorly armed Irish rebels, overmatched by the Redcoats, carried as their only food seeds of grain. At next Easter the widows and orphans made their pilgrimage to the mass burial ground where the British had thrown the unmarked bodies. As the group approached the site a little boy traveling ahead came back and said, "Mither, Mither, I've found them. Look yonder—look where the green is rising." And so I toast the rising of the green.

Anyone with a little research can come up with the right story for a toast. In 1973 a lawyer colleague of mine, Joseph Bongiovanni, Jr., then Chancellor of the Philadelphia Bar Association, and I went to Rome to extend an invitation to the people of Italy to attend the Philadelphia Bicentennial in 1976. After searching through autograph houses, I found an appropriate gift—a signed letter from William Paca, the only Italian-ancestored signer of the Declaration of Independence. The presentation of the letter to President Leone prompted a reception by him for us at Palazzo Quirinale. (Our research was not unrewarded.) To answer the toast to America by President Leone, Joe Bongiovanni told this story:

> Once Count Sforza met in New York State an Italian-American by the name of Matthews who said he changed his name from Mazzei. Sforza reprimanded him for giving up the heritage of his great name. Count Sforza reminded him that Philip Mazzei was the mentor and friend of Thomas Jefferson. Philip Mazzei, whose words Jefferson called the inspiration of the Declaration, left America in 1783 for Italy. Saying goodbye he wrote to James Madison, a later President, saying, "I am about to depart, but my heart remains behind."

Perhaps my most moving toast was at the English-Speaking Union a few years ago. I took as my source the last time Dwight David Eisenhower saw Winston Churchill. It was in August, 1964, and General Eisenhower had just finished a round of ceremonies celebrating the twentieth anniversary of the D-Day landing at Normandy. With his son John, he crossed the Channel to England, where he paid a call to Lady Churchill, at 20 Hyde Park Gate. He then inquired if her husband, then in his ninetieth year—ailing in King Edward's Hospital—was up to a visit. Assured that it would mean so much, General Eisenhower went to the hospital room. There propped up against the pillows was this old warrior, his right hand resting on the bedside table. When Churchill, too feeble to speak, raised his hand slightly to greet him, General Eisenhower went over and clasped his hand. For three—then five—then ten minutes—no words—two old men representing the best in the English-speaking world just holding hands.

Finally Churchill unclasped the hand and with his fingers in a V he waved goodbye. Eisenhower, moments later in the hospital corridor, turned to his son, who had been waiting at the door. With tears on his face he said, "I just said goodbye to Winston."

And I ended: "So: To that handclasp between those two gallant leaders and great countries which symbolized the warmth, affection, and greatness of the English-Speaking Union."

CHAPTER 6

The Speaker as Moderator

"He that puts on a publick Gown must put off a
private Person."

THOMAS FULLER

The best moderator I ever saw for a panel was a judge from
my home town of Williamsport, Pennsylvania. His name is
Charles Greevy—Judge of the Common Pleas Court of Lycom-
ing County. What makes Judge Greevy so effective in a role as
a moderator is that he is both firm and friendly. Those are the
two qualities so necessary in running a good panel session. Now
my own father was a judge in the same court as Judge Greevy.
He was also a highly respected, as well as widely popular, jurist.
But, since my father died when I was eight, I hardly remember
him. I do, though, retain a strong impression of Judge Greevy
even though I moved away from Williamsport some ten years
ago.

Charlie Greevy is a man who blends authority with affability.
He presides over a meeting as he would court. He knows his
own position without being pompous. He is warm without being weak. No doubt his career experience has trained him well
for any role like that of a moderator. He has sat over thousands
of trials and hearings. So he knows how to use his authority as
a moderator in a panel session to stop a speaker who is digress-
ing or quiet a heckler who is interrupting. Yet, on the other
hand, Charlie Greevy is a politician in the best sense of the
word. He was first elected to the judgeship. Though a Demo-
crat, he won that election by cross-filing and winning in the

Republican primary as well as the Democratic. He won because the voters sensed that Charlie would be a judge who would always have time to listen to a person's problems. Twenty-five years later he is still living up to their ideals of what a judge should be—firm, fair, and full of compassion.

A great judge must be more than a legalist who enforces the adherence to rules and procedure. He must know how to make laws come alive by applying them with a measure of human insight. He knows that black robes are sometimes brightened by a twinkle of humor and a smile of understanding.

In the same way a moderator has to govern as well as enliven a meeting. He must be ready to take charge of the session when the discussion wanders and then recharge it when it lags. Or, to put it another way, you should be enough of a general to run a meeting efficiently and should have enough general subject familiarity to inject a human or even humorous note. Now you may not feel you are the "genial general" or "jovial judge" type, but I am going to show you how in ten easy steps.

The actor John Barrymore once said, "I'm more 'broke' than the Ten Commandments." Well, if you don't want a meeting to go bust or flat, you are going to have to obey the Ten Commandments of Commanding a Meeting.

I. Thou shalt state clearly the purpose of the session. Is it to find the best rehabilitation for drug addicts or to predict trends in next year's economy? The contemporary philosopher Irving Kristol wrote, "Part of every solution is to state the problem correctly." You can't be like Alice, who asks the Cheshire-Cat for directions. The cat said, "That depends a good deal on where you want to get to." "I don't much care where," said Alice. "Then it doesn't matter which way you go," said the cat. A moderator has to have a clear conception of where the session is going to lead. Before the session even begins, he must have a general picture of the outcome of the conference's discussions. The moderator is then a "surveyor." In the very opening of the session he maps out to the panelists and participants the purpose and goal of the meeting.

What can be disastrous to any meeting is a mental situation

like that facing a certain psychiatric patient. He said to his psychiatrist, "I have this terrible problem with forgetfulness." The doctor asked, "How long have you had this problem?" To which the man replied, "What problem?" Now you may ask how an audience could forget the title of a session topic when it is printed in the program? Well, it is easy when panelists digress from the charted course. That is why the moderator in the very beginning must, in an opening paragraph, survey the ground that is going to be covered.

II. Thou shalt eliminate any foreseeable mechanical or logistical difficulties before hand. The moderator, like the director of a television show, has to make sure the panelists arrive on time. Then, after he checks the microphones and scans the programs for mistakes, he has the responsibility for starting the program on time.

A good moderator takes pains like the celebrated restaurateur César Ritz. When he was manager of London's Savoy Hotel, he was paid this compliment by one of London's most celebrated courtesans. As Ritz passed by her table, she stopped the Swiss hotel genius to give him these words of praise, "You know, Monsieur Ritz, both of us have achieved the ultimate in our respective professions." "Yes," replied Ritz, "but I have attained it with much more trouble and much less pleasure."

Similarly, the moderator like the good maître d' not only has to welcome guests but also has to make sure every table is set up in a proper fashion—that everything from ashtrays to flowers is there in place one minute before noon.

III. Thou shalt lay the proper base of expertise for each panelist. Years ago in my home area of upstate Pennsylvania a young doctor who had just finished his residency returned to the village of his birth. There he called on an old family physician. "I suppose you intend to specialize," said the old country doctor. "Oh, yes," replied the young man, "in the diseases of the nose; for the ears and throat are too complicated to be combined with the nose for purposes of study and treatment." Thereupon the family physician inquired, "Which nostril are you concentrating on?"

Now specialization may seem absurd in that case, but in a seminar you might want a panelist or speaker to concentrate on one aspect of the problem. In a discussion of the economy one speaker might dwell on the stock market and another on Detroit and the motor industry. For a workshop on urban problems, there may be an expert on housing, another on crime, and a third on mass transit. The important thing for the moderator is to make sure he qualifies each speaker as an expert in his field. The French philosopher Montaigne said, "Every expert should be believed in his own field." Well, the penalogist won't be so readily believed to be an expert if you as a moderator don't recite in your introduction his doctorate in sociology and his experience as a state consultant to two state prisons. In lecture halls a dais was built not only so speakers could be better seen but also to invest them with a measure of higher authority. If the moderator does not list the qualifications of the panelist, he is taking away that base and putting him on the same footing as the audience.

One of the key assignments of the moderator is to be an effective introducer. As introducer he doesn't have to mention that the next panelist Dr. Williamson is a devoted family man or good golfer. What he does have to do, however, is to announce what aspect of today's session Dr. Williamson will address his remarks to and how his background uniquely qualifies him for such a role. Remember that any base of expertise usually has three legs like a stool; first, the speaker's educational training; second, his professional experience or background; and third, his present assignment and title:

> In today's discussion of the U.S. foreign policy, Mr. Humes is well qualified to talk on the Mid-East crisis. His academic background was in history and the law. Two years of his education were spent abroad in England and in Spain. He adds to that a background of two years as a White House adviser and two years as Director of Policy and Plans of the State Department's Bureau of Public Affairs. Presently in private practice in Philadelphia, Mr. Humes serves on the board of the World Affairs Council and as a director

of the International Energy Institute. He also serves as a consultant to the U.S. Department of Treasury on Saudi Arabia.

IV. Thou shalt not let the panelists stray from the topic. Three years ago I came in late to a conference in Pittsburgh. I asked a man who was coming out of the hotel ballroom, "Has the Congressman begun speaking yet?" "Yes," replied the man, "he has been speaking for half an hour." "What is he talking about?" I asked. "I don't know. He hasn't said yet." Well, when a panelist digresses too far from his assigned area, it reflects not only on him but on the moderator. This is a situation where the moderator needs to have a judge's firm hand to steer the talk back on the track. When a moderator is forced to interrupt a wandering talker, he should do it with as gentle a touch as possible. "If I may interrupt. I know the audience would be fascinated by your experience in the Holmesburg prison riot. Could you share with us some of your insight on that incident?"

Erasmus wrote, "There is a great difference between speaking much and to the point." And if a speaker hasn't yet gotten to the point halfway through his allotted time, it is time for the moderator to expedite things. Run through in your own mind the speaker's background and experience and then look for the first appropriate time to break in. "You will excuse me, doctor, but your mention of De Gaulle makes me want to ask what the French and other Europeans think of our foreign policy." There is no more difficult job for the moderator than his role as an expediter—keeping the train of talk on the track.

V. Thou shalt not let a panelist speak over his limit. Once when an Illinois Congressman in the midst of a three-hour speech in the House of Representatives paused to say, "Gentlemen, I speak for posterity," Henry Clay chimed in, "And you seem determined to speak until the arrival of your audience."

As soon as a speaker approaches his time limit he should be warned. Sometimes moderators have on hand a folded cardboard card which reads, "One minute left," and another which reads, "Time's up." These messages can be passed or flashed to the speaker by the moderator.

Thomas Edison was once introduced as the great inventor. The chairman gave an exhaustive account of his many inventions—particularly the marvelous talking machine, as the phonograph was then called. Finally the introducer sat down. Edison rose and said, "I thank the chairman for his kind remarks, but I must make one correction. God invented the talking machine. I only invented the first one that can be turned off." Well, sometimes it is better to have a device to turn off the human machine. The best device is a microphone-shaped timer that fits on the podium. The timer has three lights—the top is green and says "TALK." The middle one is yellow and says "SUM UP." It goes on automatically three minutes before the end. The bottom light is red and reads "STOP." When a speaker starts to go thirty seconds overtime, it can be set to flash on and off. The advantage of a mechanical device is its impersonality. The moderator does not have the disagreeable task of interrupting and turning off a speaker.

VI. Thou shalt make sure all panelists contribute and participate. In many seminar sessions there is no time schedule. Three or four experts are gathered together to discuss a certain topic —say crime prevention. At the head table is a district attorney, a minister active in juvenile work, and a policeman. The policeman may feel he is not as articulate as the speech-trained lawyer or minister. Yet his observations on the beat could be the most meaningful. It is up to the moderator to make sure he has an opportunity to speak.

In 1975 I visited the Balfour family in Scotland. (I had stayed with them as a schoolboy.) The Earl of Balfour's daughter, Lady Evelyn, had then recently married. In talking with her and her husband Michael Brander last spring I modestly told them of my activities practicing law, lecturing, and writing a few books. As I was leaving I noticed a book on the Scottish Lowlands by Michael Brander. I asked Lady Evelyn, "Is this Michael's?" "Yes," she said. "Oh," I said, "has he written other books?" "Yes, fourteen, I think." "Oh, I didn't know Michael was a writer." "Well, you never asked."

VII. Thou shalt not take sides. Lyndon Johnson once told the story of a frontier judge in New Mexico when the state had just been admitted to the Union and the first court session opened in the new state. The judge, a grizzled old cowboy, took his place on the bench. The first case charged a man with horse stealing. After much hemming and hawing the wheels of the law began turning slowly and the plaintiff and the witnesses were heard. "Now, Judge, Your Honor," said the attorney for the defendant, "I would like to present my client's side of the case." The old judge squirted a stream of tobacco juice at the stove, cleared his throat, and said, " 'Twon't be worthwhile; it'd only confuse the jury." In panel sessions the moderator cannot use his judgelike role to shift audience sentiment toward a particular panelist. He can't take the side of the tenants' association against the real-estate man. He should not seem to sympathize with the public defender's contention against the representative from the district attorney's office. The moderator is an arbitrator, not an advocate. He can bring a panelist out without bringing to bear his opinions on the issue. He should edit without editorializing.

VIII. Thou shalt add a human touch to the proceedings. One time Senator Chauncey Depew was given a laudatory introduction. As the introducer piled on phrase after phrase describing his unique qualifications, his service to humanity, his devotion to the highest ideals, his ability, his character, finally Depew's wife, despairing of the unending encomium, leaned over and said to him in a stage whisper, "Hello, God."

Sometimes when proceedings seem too formal and stuffy, the moderator has to bring the meeting back to earth with a good story or anecdote. William Howard Taft, shortly after he was elected President, was treated to a bureaucrat's dissertation on what he called "the machinery of government." When he left, Taft said to a friend, "You know that poor fellow really thinks it is machinery and not people."

Most moderators like to open their welcome speech with a humorous story to break the ice. After all, in most of these sessions, the members of the audience are not groups like Rotarians or Presbyterians. They do not know each other. That is all the more reason to make them laugh and shed the constraints of unfamiliarity. The story should not be told just because it is funny. It should relate in some way to the proceedings —the topic, time of year, the hotel room, or the host organization. It doesn't even have to be hilariously funny if it is a warm human-interest story or a tale from history. One story I have told to begin sessions is this:

> Our country today is like the story of the late Supreme Court Justice Oliver Wendell Holmes, who once found himself on a train, but couldn't locate his ticket. While the conductor watched, smiling, the eighty-eight-year-old Justice Holmes searched through all his pockets without success. Of course, the conductor recognized the distinguished justice. So he said, "Mr. Holmes, don't worry. You don't need your ticket. You will probably find it when you get off the train and I'm sure the Pennsylvania Railroad will trust you to mail it back later." The justice looked up at the conductor with some irritation and said, "My dear man, that is not the problem at all. The problem is not where my ticket is. The problem is, where am I going?"

But as helpful as a good story may be to relax an audience at the beginning of a session, sometimes it is needed more in the middle to wake them up. The moderator should look for opportunities between panelists to tell a story—particularly one that turns on some unexpected incident in the program proceedings or on some remark that the previous speaker has just made. In that sense, the moderator plays emcee or toastmaster, with a light touch that keeps the audience in good spirits as they sit through a whole afternoon.

IX. Thou shalt field questions appropriately. During World War II the British Ambassador Lord Halifax was traveling through Texas and stopped at a factory in Fort Worth to address the workers. The man who introduced him seemed to be a bit confused as to just how he should refer to the titled envoy. He managed to get through beautifully until his closing remark, which was "When the speech is over, if anyone wants to ask questions, the Lord will provide the answers."

Well, some questions even the Lord would find difficult to

answer. The job of the moderator is to sort out those questions from the audience which are constructive and not argumentative. In this role as question sorter he is better off if he insists on written questions to be passed up to the head table. In that way, the moderator can read them first and determine their appropriateness as well as which panelist they should be addressed to. It sometimes helps if he follows his public recitation of the question with a more simplified paraphrased version. (Sometimes it helps to divide long and complex questions into different parts).

In taking questions from the floor, the moderator must remember to wield his judgelike authority. He should stop hecklers and cut off self-appointed orators. In a court a judge can interrupt and halt a question that is irrelevant (meaning unconstructive), hearsay (meaning rumor), or prejudicial (meaning unfair). The good moderator does likewise.

X. Thou shalt end a program by tying it up in a neat little package. Recently a good friend, who has become single again, was going to be in Los Angeles for an extended trip and so he asked a mutual friend of ours for a few good phone numbers. The evening after he landed, he called this gorgeous redhead model who lived in Bel Air. She said she was delighted and gave him explicit directions on how to reach her apartment. "When you get to the Bel Air Plaza, take the lobby elevator to the seventh floor, turn left and look for 718. When you reach my apartment, use your right elbow to ring the buzzer. When I hear that, I can release the security catch. All you have to do is put your left shoulder to the door and kick the bottom with your right foot." "Look," said my friend, "what do you mean with all the directions calling for an elbow, shoulder, and foot?" "But surely, darling," said the young lady, "you aren't going to come empty-handed."

And in a panel session you don't want the audience to go away empty-handed. You want to tie up the presentations of the various speakers in a nice little package they can take away with them. Perhaps the most important function of the moderator is that of a summarizer. Or better yet a consolidator. In the original sense of the word, "to consolidate" meant to make something stronger by compressing it smaller. So the task of the moderator is to boil down the various presentations into one strong message.

Arthur Larson, who was a White House speech writer for President Eisenhower once told me: "Ike did not like to waste time with conferences that ran on but came to no conclusion. Neither did he like to give speeches that offered opinions but not solutions. He would always ask me when preparing for a speech, 'Arthur, what's the Q.E.D. [quod erat demonstrandum]? What do we want to leave the audience with when we're finished speaking.' "

CHAPTER 7

The Speaker as Introducer

"The introduction is descriptive and biographical. It is story telling."

LOUIS NIZER

Probably the most famous introducer of our time was Ed Sullivan in his *Show of Shows.* Sullivan, you will recall, was nicknamed "the great stone face" for his impassive introductions of his guest stars. Comedians loved to mimic his stolid features and slowly enunciated diction. But, though he was the butt of constant jokes, Sullivan is not a bad model for the aspiring "introducer."

Sullivan, you see, never tried to compete with the guest he presented. He realized his task was to tell the audience the essential facts of his guest's background and specialty that would invite the audience's anticipation.

A couple of years ago I did some co-hosting on a television show. The producers felt I was too strong a personality to be an everyday interviewer. Not only was I too big—tall as well as wide—but I had too dominant a manner. For everyday interviewing you should not come on too strong.

Take a look at your talk show celebrities—Johnny Carson, Dick Cavett, Merv Griffin, and Mike Douglas. Basically they are not imposing figures—they are almost "beige"—a good neutral background for their guests to perform against. Remember what Marshall McLuhan said about television. He thought "cool personalities" would last longer in the immediacy of your living room. Could you, for example, take Don Rickles every morning at 7 A.M.? No, that is why the *Today Show* has the pleasantly bland Jim Hartz.

Does that mean if you are a loud talker with a big frame you shouldn't be an introducer. No, of course not, but it does mean you shouldn't dress as if you are going to a horse race or bellow an introduction that the back row of an amphitheater at a national convention could hear. An introducer should not try to overshadow or outperform the speaker he introduces. His task is to boost the speaker not himself.

That doesn't mean you have to be drab and dull. There is a middle way between being flat and being flamboyant. Be enthusiastic—believe in your speaker and in the importance of what he is going to say. Ed Sullivan conveyed earnestness in his introductions; Mike Douglas exudes excitement as he presents his guests. You don't have to be colorful to be enthusiastic. You just have to be warm in your welcome, delighted that the guest has come, and excited about his message.

The great introducer is almost a cheerleader. His enthusiasm should radiate into the audience. His job is to generate applause for the speaker. How do you do that?

Well, for one thing, you don't read off a group of statistics. "Our speaker was born in 1934 in Williamsport, Pennsylvania. He attended public schools there and then went to the Hill School. . . ." A résumé is a recital of biographical facts and statistics for job employment. When it is used as an introduction, it is inducement to lack of interest and doldrums.

I mentioned in a previous chapter how I often write my own introductions when I lecture. I do it because I know that, when a résumé is requested, it is often used almost in the form in which it was sent. Once the program chairman or introducer has those typed words in front of him, he feels compelled to draft an introduction following the same chronological framework.

Some years ago an ex-boxer went to a doctor to get some relief from his insomnia. The pugilist had tried mild sedatives, but they didn't seem to work. The doctor, hesitating to prescribe a more addictive kind, said, "Look, before I prescribe this heavier injection, I want you to try an old-fashioned remedy. You may laugh, but it actually works. Try getting yourself completely relaxed and then start counting to a hundred." A few days later the old fighter came back and said, "Doctor, I can't do it. Every time I count I jump up at the count of nine."

Well, too many program chairmen can't resist starting their introduction with birth date and going on with schooling and then ending ten minutes later by listing all the memberships and boards.

To break that habit I prescribe this formula: *summarize, dramatize, crystallize.*

First, briefly "summarize" the facts of the speaker's background; don't record them all. Once President Franklin Roosevelt was called by OPA Administrator Leon Henderson. "Mr. President", said Henderson, "did you read all the memoranda I sent you?" "Read them all!" replied the President. "I couldn't even lift them."

Some years ago, Art Buchwald had an article on the "seven-minute Louvre." The idea was that if you tried to look at every object or artifact you could spend the whole day in Egyptology. Or, as I heard one distraught father from Brooklyn say to his six children in tow, "Look, kids, if you're going to stop and look at everything you ain't goin' to see nuttin'." So Buchwald interviewed the champion doers of the Louvre, who had mapped out a way to see the Mona Lisa, Winged Victory, and Venus de Milo in seven minutes.

Well, in the same way you want to pick out the significant accomplishments on the résumé and mention them quickly almost in passing. You summarize by saying, "I could tell about his many accomplishments and activities—the fact that he was elected in 1962 as Pennsylvania's youngest legislator, or that he was cited by the American Bar Association for his efforts in preventing riots in the city of Philadelphia in the summer of 1967, or that he went to the White House in 1969 as a member of the Policy Planning Section." Just pick out a few of the most impressive facts and cite them. Don't list all the schools, all the boards, or all the jobs. There is nothing more dreary.

During the Spanish American War, the tabloid publisher William Randolph Hearst sent this telegram to his on-the-spot reporter: "Send all the juicy details. Never mind the facts."

So in the second part of the introduction you want to "dramatize"—pick out some incident in your guest's career. Tell it with relish and fervor.

In introducing me a program chairman might pick as the incident the time I met Sir Winston Churchill at 10 Downing Street. He could recount with detail the story of this young American, over on an English-Speaking Union exchange scholarship, having had the chance to talk briefly with the then seventy-eight-year-old British Prime Minister.

Then after you "dramatize," you "crystallize." What does that incident tell about Humes? Does his boyhood admiration of Churchill and subsequent contact with members of his family suggest his interest in government, his fascination with history, and his love of the English language?

There you have an easy formula—*summarize* the background facts, *dramatize* one incident or accomplishment, then *crystallize* the qualities the incident revealed.

In his novel *The Honorary Consul* Graham Greene explained why the one-eyed Cyclops is often a literary symbol. "Two eyes," he writes, "take in too much, but one eye concentrates the vision or crystallizes it." So what are the qualities or traits the incident crystallizes in your mind?

When I introduced my old friend and law school classmate J. D. Williams, the outline of remarks read this way.

Summarize: *Law Review* honors
Staff of Senator Kerr
Commission—Judge Advocate General
Head of own Washington law firm

Dramatize: An Eastern investment house, in desperation, came to a thirty-year-old Oklahoma lawyer after their New York and Philadelphia law firms gave up on finding a solution on taxes. In an eleventh-hour operation, young J. D. persuades the Congress and Senate to change the terms of the tax bill. Not bad for a young Oklahoman who had just opened an office by himself for practice. With his first client he had pulled off something the Wall Street lawyers had tried and failed to do. I don't have to say that word about J.D.'s political and legal genius spread and other clients were not long in beating their way to his door.

Crystallize: Two qualities: a brilliant legal mind combined with astute political judgment.

What is the occasion? Is the man you are about to introduce going to address the World Affairs Council on the problem of multinational corporations or is he just going to say a few light remarks to the War of 1812 Society?

In presenting my friend Victor Lang, I was quite brief,

The accomplishments of my good friend Victor Lang are both many and varied. Suffice it to say that he is a graduate of the University of Texas, with wide experience in government both at the state level in Austin and at the federal level in Washington. Presently he is vice president of International Utilities International.

But in looking over his long list of activities, I find three that pose some puzzlement and inquiry. First, he is a member of the Galveston Artillery Society, and second, he is an admiral of the Texas Navy, and third, he is a member of the French order Chevalier de Tastevin.

Now, what I want to know is this—how does one rolling caissons over land become an admiral on the water; and second, how does experience on the water make you an expert on wine?

Now there in a matter of twenty seconds I summarized, dramatized, and crystallized.

For the Philadelphia *Inquirer* and *Bulletin* I often do book reviews of biographies. The editor gave this advice. First, give a brief summation of the man's life. Then center on the author's treatment of one incident and compare that to how others have handled it. And finally, boil down your criticism to a few observations for the reader's benefit.

In the same way, if you want to use the biographical treatment in an introduction, try summarizing, dramatizing, and crystallizing. But there are various methods for clever introductions. Some like an anecdote to start off. Others rely on selected quotations. In the words of Montaigne, "I quote others only in order to express myself." Sometimes an apt quotation establishes a framework on which an introduction can be built.

Once I introduced Senator Hugh Scott to a Bar Association function this way:

> Hugh Scott is more than just the senior Senator from Pennsylvania and the Republican Minority Leader. He is a lawyer and a linguist, an author and a scholar. To sum up this many-sided man, I am forced to use the introduction Clement Attlee once made of Winston Churchill. "Churchill," he said, "is like a cake. One layer is certainly seventeenth century. The eighteenth in him is obvious. Then was the nineteenth century, and a large slice, of course, of the twentieth century, and another curious layer which may possibly have been the twenty-first."
>
> Similarly, Hugh Scott, in his rare collection of Chinese porcelain of the Cheng-te and Ming dynasties, is sixteenth or even fifteenth century. Yet, on the other hand, his reverence for the Constitution and his book on bailments suggests a Blackstonian eighteenth-century English man. As a native of Virginia and a collateral descendant of Zachary Taylor, the last plantation owner to be president, he has a quaint nineteenth-century sense of courtesy and grace. And yet how could you say he is twentieth century? He served as a naval officer in World War II, and then successfully persuaded General Eisenhower to come home from Europe and run for President in 1952. In this century he has served Presidents both with discerning loyalty and constructive opposition. And in those years one glimpses —as in Churchill—a vision of the future—of the twenty-first century, whether it be in election reform or in better environment. So might I conclude with this description De Gaulle made of Churchill, "He is the man of the day before yesterday and the day after tomorrow."

In introducing my friend Dr. Charles Wolferth, a Philadelphia surgeon, I opened this way:

Three of the greatest physicians who ever lived had this to say about their profession. First, a Philadelphian named Benjamin Rush said, "I was an advocate of principles in medicine." In the maintenance of such medical ideals, I know of no doctor who has a higher sense of commitment and dedication than Charlie Wolferth.

Then a Canadian, Sir William Osler, wrote, "The great physician cares more about the individual patient than for the special nature of the disease." In this regard also, Charles conveys, along with the science of a surgeon, the feeling of a friend.

And finally, the father of all doctors, Hippocrates, said, "The physician must have at his command a certain ready wit and sense of humor." Now, if you knew Charlie and I do—you could attest to that quality. So, command of wit, compassion, and conscience—what does that mean? It means that Charlie never takes himself too seriously, but he does take seriously his patients and his profession.

My friend Trevor Armbrister is a writer. I introduced him to a service club this way:

In a cemetery in Princeton, New Jersey, there is a gravestone inscription: "He told the truth about his century. He was a professional —he wrote honestly and well." That inscription was written for a man who wrote fiction. Yet it equally applies to one today who writes nonfiction. It describes someone who writes pieces for *The New Yorker* and *Esquire* but it also fits someone who has done articles for the *Saturday Evening Post* and *Reader's Digest*. The subject of the epitaph was the novelist and short-story writer John O'Hara, but it could also be written of the reporter and journalist Trevor Armbrister.

For Trevor in his many articles and his books on the *Pueblo* incident and the Yablonski murder case is a true professional. Never has he ever sensationalized one sentence or fictionalized one fact. For him truth is never to be sacrificed or integrity compromised.

At a reception in Washington, I presented Senator Vance Hartke with this story:

In 1951 Winston Churchill, coming back into office the second time, decided to visit Cyprus to inspect the NATO defenses. In Cyprus he was to meet for the first time Archbishop Makarios—the political leader of the island. On the plane trip Churchill turned to Defense

Minister Macmillan and said, "Harold, what type of man is this Makarios? Is he one of those priestly ascetic men of the cloth concerned only with the rewards of the spiritual hereafter, or is he one of those crafty, scheming prelates concerned rather with material advantage?"

"Well, Winston," said Macmillan, "regrettably, the Archbishop seems to be one of the latter." "Good," said Churchill, slapping his hands. "Then he is one of my kind. I can work with him." Churchill knew that constructive negotiation or progressive legislation comes not from sanctimonious saints but from pragmatic politicians. Vance Hartke is such a professional—whose skill in the arts of compromise and strategy have made him an effective force in the halls of Congress.

But, whether you use a quote or anecdote or whether you summarize, dramatize, and crystallize, by all means prepare.

An introduction looks easy. You just say a few words about the speaker and subject of his address. But because it seems so easy most people flub. When the meal is finished, the typical program chairman takes the speaker's résumé out of his coat and rises, then stumbles through the data on birth, education, and profession.

It reminds me of an initiation ceremony of an exclusive club in Oxford. The initiate would be seated at a long table with club members all around it. Before the initiate would be placed one spoon and one dish with a prune on it. The members would then watch him eat the prune. It sounds easy until you have to do it in front of everyone—then how do you eat the prune? What do you do with the pit? Do you use your hand?

And you would be surprised how people manage to foul up introductions. Judge Hastie of the Circuit Court of Appeals was formerly Governor of the Virgin Islands. I heard him once introduced as the virgin from Governor's Island.

An American toastmaster once described my British friend Sir John Wedgwood in this fashion: "He comes from a family of distinguished talent and highest honor. It would not be too much to say that the record of this family has been one of unbroken blemish."

Another British friend of mine, Jeremy Uniacke, was introduced at an English-Speaking Union fête in the Waldorf Astoria. The toastmaster mispronounced his name, saying, "It is now my honor to present Mr. Jeremy Eunuch." My friend Jeremy rose with a falsetto voice and piped, "Here."

So in making introductions first get the name straight, then put the résumé away and talk from your heart: what he does, how you met him, why you like him.

CHAPTER 8

The Speaker as Honoree

> "Man's speech should be like his life."
>
> SOCRATES

I have a theory about people—that all people are divided into two categories, the "huggable" and "crustaceans." A "huggable" person tends to wear his heart on his sleeve. He has an aura of infectious radiance about him. And, because he is vulnerable, you just want to—well—hug him. "Crustaceans," on the other hand, have shells—shells that protect their innermost feelings.

Now, while we all fall closer to one category or the other, there are times when we become more huggable or lovable. Those are the situations when we do expose our innermost self —our dreams, our likes, our hopes, our regrets.

One of these occasions is when we are honored. When that gift or plaque is presented to you, they don't want you to advocate a bill or lecture on law. They just want you to say a few words—to be yourself. That is the time to shed the judge's robe or executive's mantle. Let the audience see the real you underneath. That's what they would like to see.

When an association goes to the trouble of organizing a dinner for you, you don't have to prove yourself to that group. You already have their respect and esteem. But what you should do is let them know you a little bit better. Give them the chance to get inside you. Share with them your hopes and dreams. Express your feelings.

Some years ago the Duke and Duchess of Windsor were posing for a photograph in their suite at the Waldorf Astoria. After one shot, the photographer said, "Please, don't look so stiff. You are the most romantic couple of this century—the King who gave up his throne for the woman he loved. They are history's most magic moments. Relive them." In the next picture the Duke and Duchess looked twenty years younger. The shell had been pierced, and the inner selves were glimpsed.

When you rise to respond to a tribute, you shouldn't make a political appeal or civic talk. You don't have to play candidate or community leader. You should be yourself. Ralph Waldo Emerson once wrote, "The only gift is a portion of thyself." And the best way to repay the audience's appreciation of your work and accomplishments is to give them a bit of yourself.

In Joseph Heller's novel *Something Happened* the main character, Robert Slocum, says, "I know at last what I want to be when I grow up. When I grow up I want to be a little boy."

Is there anything more huggable than a little boy as you give him an ice-cream cone? Or how about the way your daughter looked when she opened her present of her first "crying" doll? A jet-set beauty can say, "Dahling, the diamonds were magnificent," but she still isn't huggable like that little girl. So let the audience see the little boy in you—the little-boy eagerness and enthusiasm.

Pat Weaver of NBC once interviewed President Eisenhower with this longish question, "Mr. President, you've been blessed with many things. You had a happy boyhood, fine parents, a West Point education, a wonderful wife and a fine son. You've been Supreme Commander of the greatest military force in history and the liberator of Western Europe and maybe Western Civilization. You headed a great university and now you're President of the United States. Is there anything else you'd like to be?" Ike thought for a moment and then said, "Yes, I'd like to be my grandson David."

What made Ike so popular in the affections of millions of Americans was that boyish grin. On many occasions I met and talked with General Eisenhower. He was, in conference, every inch a general—a tough, no-nonsense executive who wanted facts without embellishment. With eyes piercing and mouth pursed, he could be stern, even brusque. But, when he walked outside the office to accept the greetings of well-wishers, the twinkle returned to the eye, and the smile to the face. When he relaxed and became that little boy from Kansas, he had a glow that would light up New York in a power failure.

The secret of such an appeal is to be yourself. Maybe you aren't the little boy from Abilene who became President, but you were the little boy from somewhere else before you got to your present position. Let the audience see a glimpse of that side of you. Let them hear you talk about your hopes and dreams then.

I heard General Eisenhower once tell the story of his youth in Abilene: "There were two of us who were good friends. We shared our dreams and hopes. One said, 'Someday I will become President of the United States'—the other said, 'I'm going to be a pitcher for the major leagues.' " Said Ike, "I was the other."

We all have certain boyhood hopes and aspirations. The Spanish have a word for such a dream—*quemira.* King Philip V of Spain used the word when he had a stairway built around the favorite tree of his childhood so he could climb it at the age of sixty.

In John Knowles's book *A Separate Peace* he writes, "Everyone has a moment in history which belongs particularly to him. It is the moment when his emotions achieve their most powerful sway over him. . . . The world, through his unleashed emotions, imprinted itself upon him, and he carries the stamp of that passing moment forever."

Do you have that moment—your news of winning the scholarship, your first job, when you proposed? Can you open the curtain to one magic scene of your life?

In my own life I can remember the first time I felt like a man. I was eighteen and in London. I had just picked up and put on my first tailor-made three-piece suit—a pin-striped one. There in my Savile Row suit I met in a bank an American girl, a couple of years older, who was over from Smith College for the summer. I asked her for a date and she accepted. I knew just the place I was going to take her—an Italian restaurant in Soho

LEARNING RESOURCE CENTER
Fort Steilaccom
Community College
Tacoma, WA 98498

where you dropped coins from the balcony to musicians who played Neapolitan songs below. Now I can't even remember the girl or her name. But what I do remember is walking down Piccadilly and thinking of not just the evening but my whole life ahead. I was a man and the whole world lay before me.

You see, the scene doesn't have to be profound, but it should be intimate. When you open up a bit of your private life to them, it shows the audience that it is special.

When I was a state legislator I once invited a group of ward leaders and their wives to my house for dinner just after my daughter was christened. To share with them a private moment was the greatest thanks I could give for their work in my behalf.

So often we wear our public faces, but as an honoree you should wear your private face. As speakers we, most of the time, have a dais or platform on which we speak. In a sense it helps to increase our authority or credentials as well as the audience's ability to hear us. But as honoree you must figuratively descend from that stage and share with your listeners.

What the audience most wants from the man they honor is to see the man offstage. They want to be included in. They want to see beyond the college president, the corporation executive, or the Senator, to see the private person.

I once heard the actress Helen Hayes respond to a tribute by telling of her romance with her late husband, Charles MacArthur. She told how, while a struggling playwright, he proposed during a walk to a bench in Central Park. There he took out a bag of peanuts and said, "Gee, darling, I wish these were diamonds." A half century later, the cancer-ridden MacArthur took her again to the same park bench and gave her another bag—this time of diamonds, and he said, "Gee, darling, I wish these were peanuts."

When you share a memory or a dream with the audience, you are, in a sense, stepping off stage to say a few words to old friends. That is the secret of being an honoree.

Earlier I said an honoree should be a "huggable." Well, "huggable" is another word for "embraceable." It means to let people become part of your life—to include them in. There are two ways for the honoree to let the audience come closer to him. The first is to show appreciation for what they have done for him and the second is to share some personal recollection or reflection. That is the formula for an honoree's remarks—appreciation and reflection.

The French author Jacques Maritain wrote, "Gratitude is the most exquisite form of courtesy." Yet too often even the greatest lack the proper manners. We expect such a lack from boors but not from our bosses.

The lawyer Samuel Leibowitz saved seventy-eight accused killers from the electric chair but he claims not one of them ever sent a thank-you note or a Christmas card. A "thank you" is little enough reward for those who have taken the trouble to organize or even attend the dinner in your honor. But if the "thank you" is just a cliché—words spoken in rote without substance behind them—it is not enough. There is a way to show appreciation and that is to include them. Make them part of your triumph or success.

What you do is to make your success the audience's success, your accomplishment their accomplishment. Now it takes more than just a sentence to deflect the tribute back to the audience. You can't just say, "I couldn't have done it without you." You have to say why. Spell out briefly why the workers in the audience were the ones who got you elected. Talk about the whole team effort—whether it be the bar association or an entire company.

Once I heard an ambassador accept an award from his staff at a dinner. He told the story of how Queen Victoria never looked behind her to see if there was a chair when she wanted to sit down. It was always there. It was the concerted effort of a team behind him that made him look so good. The point is that a man who is really thankful will turn appreciation for him into appreciation for his audience and supporters.

Not long ago I heard a scientist accept an award for research in biomedicine. He said in acceptance, "I feel very much like

Isaac Newton, who said when receiving a tribute, 'If I have seen farther, it is because I had the chance to stand on others' shoulders.' "

There are those in the audience who lifted you up. Single them out. Let them share in the evening celebration.

My friend Donald Whitehead—Federal Co-Chairman of the Appalachian Regional Commission—was once given an award for the efforts of the commission in Appalachia. To the audience, which was mostly comprised of local officials who were part of the structure of the commission, Don said, "I feel a little like President Lincoln when one of his supporters said, 'God Almighty and Abraham Lincoln have saved this country.' Lincoln laughed and said, 'My friend, you are half right.' And you are half right when you praise the work of me and the commission."

My friend Jim Greenlee, a lawyer, once got an award from the Junior Chamber of Commerce. He accepted the citation with these remarks: "Nicholas Murray Butler, the president of Columbia University once said, 'You have two choices before you: you can either get the job done or get the credit for doing it. You can't do both.' Well, tonight I am getting the credit, so you and I know who really got the job done—it was a lot of you out there. . . ."

Now, once the honoree has shown appreciation, then it is time for reflection—a little personal reminiscing or dreaming aloud. By both "appreciation" and "reflection" you bring the audience closer around you. First you let them share your success and then you let them share your dreams.

A few years ago, Pablo Casals said to a group who had come to honor him, "What can I say to you? I am perhaps the oldest musician in the world, but I still want to dream young. And this is what I want you to do—dream young—be young—act young all your life and say things to the world that are true."

As in the case of Casals, sometimes the words of reflection are almost a "benediction." Listen to what the late Justice Hugo Black said just before his death to a group of Harvard Law students from Alabama who came with a presentation to his court chambers, "I congratulate you, all of you. I wish I were in your place. I can tell you from experience that it's a great world. Here's hope and strength and love to those who give hope and strength and love."

Sometimes your reflections may take on a lighter tone. Arthur Rubinstein on his eighty-seventh birthday said, "At twenty-one I found that nothing can stop us—no law, no priest, no government. Nothing can stop us from loving flowers and loving women and this I discovered at twenty-one."

In 1970 old Harve Taylor, with whom I served in the Pennsylvania legislature, was invited to the White House by President Nixon. The then ninety-four-year-old party warhorse gave to the President and other well-wishers his secret of longevity. Said Harve, "I never took a drink of liquor, I never chewed tobacco, and I never fooled around with a woman—until I was twelve years old."

President Eisenhower handled a birthday tribute in 1959 from the White House press corps a bit differently. When the presenter of the gift stated that the President, on his next birthday in 1960, would be the oldest President ever to serve, Ike made this response, "I believe it's a tradition in baseball that when a pitcher has a no-hitter going for him, nobody reminds him of it."

Wit is always appropriate in remarks of "reflection" but so is wisdom. Sometimes, what you say should, in the words of Virginia Woolf's diary, add to the vision of life.

The French writer Albert Camus in accepting the Nobel Prize in 1957 said, "The two trusts that constitute the nobility of one's service are—the service of truth and the service of freedom."

My own good friend Judge Charlie Greevy told this Biblical story when he was honored with a Brotherhood Award in 1961. "In the Old Testament, we remember how King Solomon, as a youth, was visited by an angel of the Lord. The angel asked the newly anointed King what he needed most to rule—such as power or riches? What gift do you want?' And Solomon replied, 'Give me an understanding heart.'"

Whether it is a French philosopher or a Pennsylvania judge talking, the best wisdom comes in the condensed reflection of a lifetime. The painter James Whistler once brought a successful libel suit against Victorian critic John Ruskin. Ruskin had charged Whistler with "flinging a pot of paint in the public's face." "How long did it take you to paint the work?" the judge asked, to which Whistler replied, "Two hours and a lifetime."

And similarly, if your remarks are two minutes and a lifetime, they could be the most moving words you will ever say.

PART II: ROLE BITS

CHAPTER 9

The Role Player

"The voice is a second face."
GÉRARD BAUER

One who wants to be an actor these days has to be versatile to survive—musical comedy, Shakespearean tragedy, TV soap opera, experimental Off-Broadway, Hollywood film, touring road shows, or advertising commercials. He has to dig into his repertoire of roles and come up with a sterling performance of the proud father, the romantic bridegroom, the young scientist, the efficient executive, and the old grandfather.

And so do we all one time and another have to play many parts. We may be urging as an advocate or explaining as a lecturer, dedicating as a commemorator or greeting as a toastmaker, presiding as a moderator or presenting as an introducer, but whatever form our speech, we play a certain role. Goethe once said, "We accept every person in the world as that for which he gives himself out, only he must give himself out for something." That is to say, life makes us put on many masks—we act as wise teachers, dedicated civic leaders, concerned politicians, or even romantic husbands. Maybe we are not all those things, but the audience accepts our performance because they know we are doing it with a purpose in mind—a father at a wedding, a civic leader at a United Fund drive, a husband at an anniversary.

But unlike actors we have no scripts before us. We sometimes find it difficult to put our feelings into words. We sometimes wish we had something to get us started—maybe a quote or a story. As Horace wrote, "Once begun a job is easy—half the work is done."

So I have gathered here for you some opening lines for most of life's roles—be it winner or lover, parent or patriot. The lines may not end your preparations, but they may represent as Churchill once said, "not the end, nor the beginning of the end, but . . . perhaps the end of the beginning."

At a dinner in Hollywood, Charlie Chaplin entertained the guests throughout the evening by imitating people they knew: men, women, and children, his chauffeur, his Japanese servants, his secretaries. Finally he sang at the top of his voice an aria from the Italian opera *Pagliacci*. He sang it superbly. "Why, Charlie, I never knew you could sing so beautifully," someone exclaimed. "I can't sing at all," Chaplin replied. "I was only imitating Caruso."

Similarly, you may be fearful about mounting the podium or rising to toast, but if you just remember to play the role and not yourself, it's easy.

ACTOR

1   What did Walter Winchell once write—"They shoot too many pictures and not enough actors"? Well, here is one actor who has survived.

2   A columnist once described the rise and fall of a movie star:

> Who is Hugh O'Brian (name any actor)?
> Get me Hugh O'Brian!
> Get me a Hugh O'Brian type!
> Get me a younger Hugh O'Brian!
> Who is Hugh O'Brian?

Well, we can be sure they will never ask who is ———?

3   Oscar Levant once described the movie world, "Strip the phony tinsel off Hollywood and you'll find the real tinsel underneath."

4   As John Barrymore once observed, "If you stay in front of that camera long enough, it will show you not only what you had for breakfast, but who your ancestors were."

5   The Italian playwright Luigi Pirandello described the theater this way, "What is the stage? It's a place, you know, where people play at being serious." Well, I now propose we be serious at playing . . .

6   I sometimes feel the way Spencer Tracy did when Lee Marvin was trying to discuss motivations during a scene: "I'm too old and tired for all this bullshit—so let's just do the scene." So enough of these speeches—let's get on with the action.

7   As for me I like the advice Tallulah Bankhead gave on being an actor, "All you have to know is Shakespeare, the Bible, and how to shoot craps."

8   A famous actor once said he was in a way a sculptor who carved in snow.

9   Noel Coward was once asked for the secret of his great talent as an actor. "I speak," he replied, "in a loud, clear voice and try not to bump into the furniture."

ACTRESS

10   Ethel Waters once said, "I have a spiritual suitcase and I know where I am going."

11   As Ethel Barrymore once observed—"an actress to be a success must have the face of Venus, the brains of Minerva, the grace of Terpsichore, the memory of Macaulay, the figure of Juno and the hide of a rhinoceros."

ADMIRAL

12   Lately I am seeing some of the wisdom of the Gilbert and Sullivan ditty:

> Now landsmen all, whoever you may be,
> If you want to rise to the top of the tree
> If your soul isn't fettered to an office stool,
> Be careful to be guided by this golden rule—
> Stick close to your desks and *never go to sea*
> And you all may be Rulers of the Queen's Navee.

But at least one advantage of desk duty in Washington is that you get to see more of your old friends who come in and out of here.

13   Voltaire once said, "It is good from time to time to kill an admiral in order to encourage the others."

14   In 1939 when Winston Churchill returned to the post First Lord of the Admiralty, he said, "For each and all . . . let the watchword be 'Carry on and dread naught.'"

ADVERTISING EXECUTIVE

15   Bruce Barton, one of the early great advertising men, used to say to his staff at BBDO: "When you're through changing, you're through." Today we must ask ourselves in what ways we have fallen behind.

16   What did Fred Allen say about an advertising agency —85 percent confusion and 15 percent commission? Well, the way I got into advertising was about 15 percent decision and about 85 percent drifting.

17   In a way, doing a business without advertising is like winking at a girl in the dark. You know what you are doing but nobody else does.

18   Most advertising men believe the Apostle Paul's words, "For if the trumpet give an uncertain sound, who shall prepare himself to the battle?" The secret of advertising is a simple message that everyone can understand and respond to —and I hope you will respond to this.

19   More than a century and a half ago the French writer Alexis de Tocqueville, wrote down the basic principle of communication: "A false notion which is *clear* and *precise* will always have more power in the world than a true principle which is *obscure* and *involved.*" So today I would like to boil down our message to one phrase . . .

20   Franklin D. Roosevelt said, "If I were starting my life all over again, I am inclined to think that I would go into the advertising business in preference to almost any other. This is because advertising has come to cover the whole range of human needs and also combines real imagination and a deep study of human psychology. Because it brings to the greatest number of people actual knowledge of useful things, it is an essential form of education. The general raising of the standards of modern civilization among all groups of people during the past half century would have been impossible without the spreading of the knowledge of higher standards by means of advertising." I know advertising men are not high on everyone's list of respected vocations. I like to remember what Winston Churchill said: "Advertising nurses the consuming power of man. It creates wants for a better standard of living. It sets before man the goal of a better home, better clothing, better food for himself and his family. It spurs individual exertion and greater production."

21   The first rule I learned in advertising is you always speak the truth unless you are an exceptionally good liar.

22   It was Robert Louis Stevenson who predicted the age of mass media—he said soon men will not live on bread alone but by catchwords.

23   Advertising genius David Ogilvy once told a group of copywriters, "The consumer is not a mass. She's your wife."

24   Adolph Ochs of the *New York Times* once observed: "Advertising in the final analysis should be news. If it is not news it is worthless."

25   Henry Ward Beecher once said, "The advertisements in a newspaper are more full of knowledge in respect to what is going on in a state or community than the editorial columns are."

26   Anne Morrow Lindbergh commented that "good communication is stimulating as black coffee, and just as hard to sleep after."

27   In this instance I am reminded of a saying by Confucius: "If language be not in accordance with the truth of things, affairs cannot be carried on to success."

28   Carl Sandburg said that "slang is a language that rolls up its sleeves, spits on its hands, and goes to work."

29   On the subject of public relations, Alan Harrington remarked that "public-relations specialists make flower arrangements of the facts, placing them so that the wilted and less attractive petals are hidden by sturdy blooms."

30   I think businessmen should be blowing their own horn more often, for—as W. S. Gilbert put it:

> If you wish in the world to advance
> Your merits you're bound to enhance
>   You must stir it and stump it
>   And blow your own trumpet.
> Or, trust me, you haven't a chance.

31   I recall the lines in *South Wind* by Norman Douglas: "You can tell the ideals of a nation by its advertisements."

AFTER-DINNER SPEAKER

32   As Dr. Samuel Johnson said to Boswell, "Depend upon it, Sir, when a man knows he is to be hanged in a fortnight, it concentrates his mind wonderfully." But tonight I had no such warning.

33   I do not object to people looking at their watches when I am speaking, but I strongly object when they start shaking them to make certain they are still going. It is late so I will be brief.

34   Winston Churchill is reported to have said that the three most difficult things for a man to do are, one, to climb a wall that is leaning toward him; two, to kiss a woman who is leaning away from him; and three, to deliver a good after-dinner speech. Since this is an after-breakfast talk, the degree of difficulty should be somewhat less.

ALUMNUS

35   As I look at this class of grads, I recall the words of William Howard Taft, "Some are graduated from college *cum laude,* some are graduated *summa cum laude,* and some are graduated *mirabile dictu.*"

36   Reunion time is the occasion when old grads return, united by one prayer—Make me a sophomore just for tonight —and often those prayers are answered.

37   Cardinal Newman wrote: "A university according to the usual designation—is not a factory or a mint or a treadmill but an Alma Mater; she knows each of her children one by one." And similarly, each of us has our single impression of our days here. I know mine . . .

38   The Spanish have a word, *saudade* which means the
hopes and dreams of youth. The Spanish poet García Lorca used
it when he wrote: "Espero las saudades de mi vida regresaran
—If only I could recapture the dreams of yesterday." Today I'd
like to go back to the times of our college days and the world
and national scene as it was then—and remember what our
hopes and dreams were. . . .

ARCHITECT

39   Goethe once called a great building "frozen music."
And the many people who deserve credit for the construction
of this edifice may be compared to the players of a symphony
orchestra—each role orchestrated in perfect symphony.

40   Edward Durell Stone once said, "I have spent fifty
years of my life trying to perpetuate the idea that the visionary
can be made visible." And today with the dedication of this
building we see the fruition of a dream.

41   Buckminster Fuller was asked whether beauty of form
was a major factor in his designing of a building. He said, "No,
I design the best possible building for the function intended.
But if, when it is done, it does not look beautiful I throw it away
and start again." I think today we have the best possible building . . .

42   It was Mies van der Rohe, the architect, who said,
"Less is more." When I look at the clean and beautiful lines of
this structure, I know what he meant.

43   A new word that fills a gap in the language was minted
by architectural writer Ada Louise Huxtable to describe a
happy marriage of form and function: "beautility." And when
you combine beauty with utility you have the essence of this
building.

44   The architect must have vision. As Ruskin wrote, "No
person who is not a sculptor or painter can be an architect. If

he is not a sculptor or painter, he can only be a builder." I can tell you that there was a vision—a concept—that preceded the blueprint.

ARTIST

45   In the fifth century Hsieh Ho of China laid down six rules of painting: (1) rhythmic vitality, (2) anatomical structure, (3) conformity with nature, (4) harmonious coloring, (5) composition, and (6) finish.

46   "Art" said André Gide, "is the collaboration between God and the artist, and the less the artist does the better."

AUDITOR

47   As Dickens' Micawber put it, "Annual income twenty pounds, annual expenditure nineteen nineteen six, result happiness. Annual income twenty pounds, annual expenditure twenty pounds ought and six, result misery." And I am happy to say the audit puts us on the happiness side of the ledger.

48   How did Persius describe the rich man? "Ever a glutton, at another's cost,/But in whose kitchen dwells perpetual frost." And today we must take a cold look at the rising costs in our kitchen.

49   It takes a good auditor to keep records that satisfy the stockholders, the income-tax authorities, and the management. I am not sure that my report . . .

50   Sir Winston Churchill once said, "Some think it is a sin to make a profit but the real sin is to take a loss." At the rate we are going, we are treading down the road to sin and perdition.

AUTHOR

51   As Dr. Samuel Johnson observed, "The greatest part of a writer's time is spent in reading, in order to write; a man will turn over half a library to make one book."

52   If you want to get rich from writing, write the sort of thing that's read by persons who move their lips when they're reading to themselves.

53   George Bernard Shaw once wrote that the hardest thing about being an author is having no office to go to—a trial, he said, of which you can have no conception.

54   Somerset Maugham wrote that only a mediocre writer is always at his best.

55   There are two literary maladies—writer's cramp and swelled head.

56   The French writer Charles Baudelaire wrote that on the day a writer corrects his first proofs he is as proud as a schoolboy who has just got his first dose of pox.

BANKER

57   The business management consultant Dr. Peter Drucker said, "The economic growth of America depends primarily on people saving money or investing it—either directly in stocks or indirectly through savings accounts. Millions of Americans risk savings in the belief that a healthy American economy will allow them to share in the profits. That profit motive is what provides jobs, builds homes, and advances our standard of living." Today I would like to talk unashamedly about the profit motive.

- Why young people reject the concept
- • Why it is downgraded in schools

••• Why businessmen must begin selling the idea of business

58   They say an investment trust is known by the company it keeps. Seriously, any trust is based on faith. Faith in people you know, their ability and integrity. And in that sense I feel we are blessed . . .

59   What a diplomat calls a treaty, what a politician calls an election promise, a banker calls unsecured paper. And I suppose another kind of unsecured paper is a story not based on statistics or facts. Today I would like to begin by citing some facts of life about our economic climate.

60   Mark Twain once said of us bankers: we are people who lend an umbrella when the sun is shining but won't lend it when it starts to rain. Actually, a better definition would be: we will lend money when we think it's going to be shining soon but won't lend it if we are predicting rain. Well, today I'm going to talk about why I think there's a sunny future before us.

61   What is that old saying by Oliver Wendell Holmes? "Put not your trust in money, but put your money in trust."

62   At the turn of the century there was a daring speculator named Charles Flint who operated in Wall Street. Once he found himself in serious financial straits, and knowing J. P. Morgan, the elder, slightly, he approached him for a loan. Mr. Morgan consented to take a stroll with him to the Battery. He talked polite nothings, however, the entire time. Finally, after about an hour, Flint blurted, "But, Mr. Morgan, how about that million dollars I want to borrow?" Morgan held out his hand to say goodbye and answered, "Oh, you won't have any trouble getting it now that we have been seen together."

BOREDOM

63   Queen Marie Antoinette in 1775, often called Madame Deficit for her extravagances, said, "I am frightened of boredom."

64   In T. S. Eliot's *Cocktail Party,* Edward asks, "What is hell? Hell is oneself, hell is alone."

65   Admiral Byrd so feared it that he took twelve straitjackets on his Antarctic expedition. Lindbergh complained of it repeatedly on his flight to Paris. Bertrand Russell wrote, "Half the sins of mankind are caused by fear of it." Erich Fromm calls it "the illness of the age," the root cause of violence and drug addiction. Boredom has always been with us. But behavioral scientists make a strong case that chronic boredom is epidemic in our industrial society. They call ours "the land of the free and the home of the bored."

BUILDER

66   We recall the story of the great French General, Marshal Lyautey, who once asked his gardener to plant a tree. The gardener demurred, "Marshal, this tree is slow growing and will not reach maturity for a hundred years." Marshal Lyautey replied, "In that case, we have no time to lose—*plant it this afternoon.*"

67   William Penn was the founder of Pennsylvania. On the base of his statue that towers over City Hall in Philadelphia is the Biblical inscription LO—I GO TO PREPARE A PLACE BEFORE THEE. Today we must prepare a place for our children and our children's children.

68   Alexander Hamilton, when a boy of twelve, was a stock clerk in a West Indies store. Impatient and restless, he despised the mediocrity of his work and yearned in his dreams for the

right outlet for his ambitions. He penned in his diary these words: "I mean to prepare the way for futurity."

BUSINESSMAN

69   In ancient Athens they had a word for men who were so involved in their own business affairs that they neglected their civic responsibilities—the word was "idiot," which meant an incomplete man, or half citizen.

- To be involved in cultural life
- •• To be involved in civic life
- ••• To be involved in political life

70   Walter Lippmann wrote, "Private property was the original source of freedom. It still is its main bulwark." In the name of equality many totalitarian societies have eroded or destroyed private property. The lesson is not lost on us today....

71   In 354 B.C. the statesman Isocrates complained, "When I was a boy it was considered an honor to be a businessman but now one must apologize for success in business as if it were an utter violation of moral law." The time has come for businessmen today to cease being on the defensive and take the offensive.

- Tell your children how you make your living
- •• Put programs on in high schools to show how our economy works
- ••• Take active interest in what is going on in Washington and State Capitol

72   The famous management consultant Dr. Peter Drucker argued recently, "Actually the profit margin on which the American economy operates is definitely too low. We will have to increase it not only to obtain the economic expansion needed for stable employment but in the interests of national strength and survival."

73   When Alexander Hamilton was helping to write the Constitution he wrote, "Not only the wealth but the Independence and Security of a country appear to be materially connected with the Prosperity of manufactures."

74   Today, to much of the public, "profit" spelled p-r-o-f-i-t is without honor and "sell" is a four-letter word. Why is business on the defensive?

75   In the nineteenth century there was the influence of Victorianism. Now there seems to be economic Victorianism. Victorians thought sex was a dirty word. Sure, sex has its exploitive side—but it is the force that builds homes and families. In economic Victorianism, "profit" is a dirty word. The profit drive, like the sex drive too, may have its darker side, but it is also the force that builds industries, jobs, and our standard of living.

76   The philosopher and educator Irving Kristol asks, "How have we managed to raise a whole generation of young people who don't know how their parents make a living?"

  • People do not understand the American economy
  •• People think profit incentive wrong

77   President Eisenhower once said, "When shallow critics denounce the profit motive in our system of private enterprise, they ignore the fact that it is an economic support of every human right we possess and without it, all rights would soon disappear."

78   Henry David Thoreau said, "It is truly enough said that a corporation has no conscience; but a corporation of conscientious men is a corporation with a conscience."

  • Obligation to its employees
  •• Obligation to consumers
  ••• Obligation to society

79   Some sixty years ago in a Midwestern city, just after Theodore Roosevelt had given a speech, a member of the audi-

ence approached the speaker's platform and said, "Mr. President, I am just an ordinary businessman. What can I possibly do to help my country?" And Theodore Roosevelt replied, "Do what you can with what you have got, where you are, but do it." What can a businessman do to make the community work better?

- No job discrimination
- • Responsibility to employees
- • • Recognize responsibility to community in which company lives

80   The Roman Emperor Marcus Aurelius said, "Never make business an excuse to decline the offices of humanity."

81   A distressing poll of high school seniors revealed these salient facts about the general ignorance of young people about the free-enterprise system.

62% believe	a worker should not produce all he can.
76% believe	the money saved by new machinery goes to the owner.
61% believe	the profit system is not essential to our way of life.

82   There are basically seven M's of business:

Money—sufficient operating cash
Management—sound leadership
Merchandise—salable product
Men—cooperative work force
Market—good distribution
Machinery—adequate facilities
Margin—normal or better profit

83   Churchill once said, "The trouble with socialism is socialism but I say the trouble with capitalism is capitalists."

84   In his *Democracy in America,* Alexis de Tocqueville wrote: "In democracies, nothing is more great or more brilliant than commerce: it attracts the attention of the public, and fills

the imagination of the multitude; all energetic passions are directed towards it."

85   Ovid, in *The Art of Love,* wrote: "A horse never runs so fast as when he has other horses to catch up and out-pace."

86   As one interested for a long time in the world of business and the world of politics I have come to two conclusions: Politicians should not advise businessmen if they don't know the difficulty of carrying a payroll. And businessmen should not advise politicians if they don't know the difficulty of carrying a precinct.

87   The man who goes into politics as a business has no business to go into politics.

88   P. G. Wodehouse in *Leave It to Jeeves* described a prevalent image of the American businessman: "From what I observed, the American captain of industry doesn't do anything out of business hours. When he has put the cat out and locked up the office for the night, he just relapses into a state of coma from which he emerges only to start being a captain of industry again."

CANDIDATE

89   Some years ago Lieutenant Governor James Blair of Missouri filed for a second term with this refreshing announcement: "There isn't any great public outcry for me to do this. I just want the office."

90   Lord Chesterfield once described politics to his son: "The pursuit of office is like the pursuit of women—the position ridiculous, the expense damnable and the pleasure fleeting." Well, however exhilarating campaigning is, it is expensive and for that . . .

91   The playwright Henrik Ibsen said, "A man should never put on his best trousers when he goes out to battle for freedom and truth." And in that spirit I pledge a fighting campaign. . . .

92   Justice Oliver Wendell Holmes said: "Life is a roar of bargain and battle—but in the very heart of it there rises a mystical spiritual tone that gives meaning to the whole. It transmutes the dull details into romance." And in this campaign I have come to perceive a sense of awareness—a dedication that makes each issue stand out in bold . . .

93   I hesitate to compare myself to Lincoln but his answer to the evangelist applies to me. When a preacher during a service asked all those who wanted to go to heaven to rise, everyone rose but Lincoln. When he asked all those who didn't want to go to hell to rise, again Lincoln stayed put. So the preacher said, "If you don't want to go to Heaven and don't want to escape Hell, Mr. Lincoln, where do you want to go?" Lincoln rose and said, "I'm going to Congress." And similarly I intend to go to Washington.

94   Of all the positions in bureaucracy the one I like best is one in AID—the Administrative Assistant to the Assistant Administrator for Administration.

95   Two hundred years ago Thomas Jefferson wrote in the Declaration of Independence about King George's bureaucracy: "He has erected a multitude of New Officers and sent the other swarms of Officers to harass our people, and eat out their substance."

96   In 1974 the Federal Budget spent tax money in some of these ways: $6,000 for a study of bisexual frogs; $25,000 for a World War I Emergency Bureau; and $832,000 to redecorate an office suite for the head of the Postal Service and stock his private dining room with crystal.

97   In one of his novels F. Scott Fitzgerald writes that optimists are contented small men in high office.

98   The word "candidate" comes from the word "candidatus," meaning those wearing the white toga of a Roman office seeker; the toga meant the aspirant was free from any preconceived solutions or biases.

99   I am told that too many campaigns are won not on ability but affability.

100   Evelyn Waugh once wrote in his diary that politicians do not seek office to attain policies—they seek policies to attain office.

101   I am reminded of the time in 1952 when Adlai Stevenson was wished luck. "Governor," the woman supporter said, "you have the vote of every thinking person." To which Stevenson replied, "That's not enough, madam, I need a majority."

102   As George Bernard Shaw once wrote, "Principles without programs are platitudes."

103   Majority Leader Tip O'Neill tells of his first political race. He was running for City Council in Cambridge. "Thomas," said Mrs. O'Brien, "I'm going to vote for you even though you never asked me to." I said, "Mrs. O'Brien, I've been shoveling your walk and mowing your grass ever since I can remember. I didn't think I had to ask you to vote for me." "Well, everyone else has," she replied. "If you want my vote, I'll give it to you. But you first got to ask."

104   In Edward Gibbon's *Decline and Fall of the Roman Empire* he describes decaying Rome this way: "The nice and artificial machinery of government was out of joint."

105   The Revolutionary patriot James Otis wrote, "The power of the Crown has increased and is increasing and ought to be diminished."

106   When I see the millions spent each day by the Federal government, I think of the old Egyptian hieroglyphic symbol for million: it was a man kneeling with his arms spread in amazement.

107   As the old Tennessee minister Parson Brownlow said in 1861, "We shall fight the secessionist leaders until hell freezes over and then, my friends, we'll fight on ice."

108   Sometimes I really don't think I'm worthy of office—but then I have to put the country ahead of my own limitations.

109   As General Eisenhower said, "I'm a moderate—a middle-of-the-roader who believes that too often at the extreme ends of either side of the road run the sewers."

110   My platform will be the three R's—not Reading, 'Riting, 'Rithmetic, but Reform, Restoration, and Renewal. Reform in government, Restoration of the environment, and Renewal of society.

111   Two British soldiers died in the skirmish at Concord Bridge. Their tomb, now part of the general shrine, bears a quatrain beginning:

> They came three thousand miles and died
> To keep the past upon its throne. . . .

To fight against that past enthroned—enthroned privileges and power—is exactly what I intend to do.

112   James Madison, a Constitutional Founding Father, once wrote prophetically: "There are more instances of the abridgment of the freedom of the people by gradual and silent encroachment of those in power than by violent and sudden usurpations."

113   In his novel *A Bell for Adano,* John Hersey describes how, after the Americans invaded Italy in World War II, officials in a small Italian village soon were similar to those officials who had abused their power under the previous regime.

114   The United States was founded on a complaint. It was, as the framers of the Declaration of Independence were at pains to point out, a reasonable complaint, and one that took time to ripen, "All Experience hath shewn, that Mankind are

more disposed to suffer, while Evils are sufferable, than to right themselves by abolishing the Forms to which they are accustomed. But when a long Train of Abuses . . ." That complaint got action. In fact, in an adversary proceeding that is the essence of democracy, every election poses a complaint and offers a remedy of sorts.

115   John Randolph, the American statesman, said to a waiter, at the same time handing him his cup and saucer: "Take that away—change it." "What do you want, Mr. Randolph?" asked the waiter. "Do you want coffee or tea?" "If that stuff is tea," said he, "bring me coffee, if it's coffee, bring me tea. I want a change."

116   As to my opponent's program, I can only say what Dr. Samuel Johnson said criticizing the recommendations of a colleague: "I found them to be good and original. However, the part that was good was not original. And the part that was original was not good."

117   An English Parliamentarian once said about British Prime Minister Gladstone: "I don't object to the old man keeping a card up his sleeve, but I do object to his asserting that God put it there."

118   Sometimes in this campaign I am reminded of what Charles de Gaulle said of Churchill: "When I am right, I get angry. Churchill gets angry when he is wrong. So we were very often angry at each other."

119   In Ecclesiastes Solomon wrote: "The race is not to the swift, nor the battle to the strong, neither yet bread to the wise, nor yet riches to men of understanding, nor yet favour to men of skill; but time and chance happeneth to them all."

120   Adlai Stevenson once remarked that "the hardest thing about any political campaign is how to win without proving that you are unworthy of winning."

121   I recall the words in Aeschylus' Greek drama *Agamemnon,* "Keep your course. Wax fat. Dishonor justice. You have power—now."

122   The government today reminds me of what Shakespeare's Buckingham said of Cardinal York:

> The devil speed him: No man's pie is freed
> From his ambitious finger.

123   At one time when Abraham Lincoln was censured for his unwavering policy in defense of the Union, he gave this answer to his critics: "I am not bound to win, but I am bound to be true. I am not bound to succeed, but I am bound to live up to what light I have. I must stand with anybody that stands right: stand with him while he is right and part from him when he goes wrong."

124   As Lincoln made his way from Springfield to Washington to be inaugurated the sixteenth President, on the special train he often made speeches from the back car to assembled citizens at various stops. At one stop, he exhorted them that the future of democracy depended on them, not him:

"I appeal to you to constantly bear in mind that not with politicians, not with presidents, not with office seekers, but with you is the question: Shall the liberties of this country be preserved to the latest generations?"

125   In 1910 in Atlantic City a political party had done the unthinkable, they nominated for Governor an academician. Many of the party pros were at first unenthusiastic when they heard him give his acceptance speech, but even many of them broke into tears when Woodrow Wilson said: "And then trust your guides, imperfect as they are, and someday when we are dead, men will come and point at the distant upland with a great shout of joy and triumph and thank God that there were men who undertook to lead in the struggle. What difference does it make if we ourselves do not reach the uplands? We have given our lives to the enterprise. The

world is made happier and humankind better because we have lived."

126   In A.D. 67 the great Apostle Paul found himself jailed in a Roman prison under Nero's edict. The great missionary now dying gave a Christian visitor Onesiphorus a message to his loyal aide and the man who was a son to him, Timothy. It was the final message from the pen whose writings changed history.

The note delivered after Paul's death to Timothy was "I have fought a good fight, I have finished my course, I have kept the faith." And so may I pledge in this campaign to keep the faith in an honest fight.

CHILDREN

127   Some of my best friends are children. In fact, all of my best friends are children.

128   The Quaker leader Dr. Rufus Jones once wrote, "The unwarped child, with his spontaneous faith and confidence in goodness, is the best illustration of that spirit which fits the Kingdom of God."

CIVIC LEADER

129   Centuries ago the Athenians used to take an oath upon reaching adulthood. It said: "We will strive unceasingly to quicken the public sense of public duty that thus we will transmit this city not less but greater and more beautiful than it was transmitted to us." Now if we took such an oath, how would we strive to leave this city for our children better than we found it?

130   Dr. Albert Schweitzer said, "There is no higher religion than human service. To work for the common good is the

greatest creed." And you work for humanity in the slums of our city as well as in the jungles of Africa.

131   The story has been told that the young William Penn was once asked by an acquaintance to take him to a Quaker meeting in London. The future founder of Pennsylvania did so. When the friend had sat through an hour of silence, he puzzledly asked Penn, "When does the service begin?" And Penn replied, "The service begins when the meeting ends."

132   In ancient Greece the legislator Solon put in a provision that when controversial political issues arose the citizens had to take sides or risk losing their citizenship. In other words, people were compelled to get involved—to take sides —to express themselves on community issues.

133   To understand why the Jewish community responds to civic appeals it is necessary to understand Hebrew. There is no exact equivalent for the English word "charity." The Hebrew word is "Tzedakah," which basically means "Whoever you are, there is someone else who needs something more than you." In other words, "Tzedakah" means "brotherhood" whereas "charity" often suggests paternalism.

134   There is a slogan for the VISTA agency that sums up the type of spirit we need: "If you are not part of the solution, you're part of the problem."

> • We are part of the problem when we don't care
> •• We are part of the problem when we don't give
> ••• We are part of the problem even if we give money but give nothing of ourselves

135   I recall a famous cartoon strip of Walt Kelly's *Pogo* in which the hero of Okefenokee swamp said, "We have met the enemy and he is us."

> • The enemy is misunderstanding
> •• The enemy is our apathy

••• The enemy is our lack of organization and commitment

136   Success does not just depend on the leadership of this campaign. We recall in Exodus how God told Moses as long as he raised his hands so the Israelites could see him, they would win in battle. But Moses became tired, his arms dropped, and the Israelites began to lose. So Aaron climbed the mountain, found a stone seat for Moses, and then held each of Moses' arms up so that the Israelites began winning again.

137   When Heinrich Heine, the great German poet, was asked how it was that people were no longer able to build the awe-inspiring cathedrals of medieval times, he replied, "In those days men had convictions. We moderns have only opinions and it requires something more than opinions to build a Gothic cathedral." And it is going to take more than opinions to put this campaign over the top. . . .

• Our message
•• Our mission
••• Our mobilization

138   It was the Frenchman Alexis de Tocqueville who said, "I have often admired the extreme skill with which the inhabitants of the United States succeed in proposing a common object for the exertions of a great many men and inducing them voluntarily to pursue it." De Tocqueville observed that in American life the most important sector was not so much the government sector or the business sector, but the volunteer sector—people voluntarily helping one another in times of community need—a barn raising when a barn burned down, a sewing bee when clothes were washed away in floods. . . .

139   In the "The Missing Three-Quarter," Sherlock Holmes says, "You may look upon me simply as an irregular pioneer, who goes in front of the regular forces of the country."

140   John W. Gardner in *The Recovery of Confidence* wrote, "The identifying of values to which we can all give alle-

giance is a light preliminary exercise before the real and heroic task: to make the values live. Values have been carved on
monuments and spelled out in illuminated manuscripts. We
do not need more of that. They must be made to live in the
acts of men."

141   King Paul of Greece once visited a group of university students who were working on rebuilding projects in
Athens. When he stopped to wield a pick with them, some of
the students shouted, "We want to die for Greece." "That's
not enough," he declared. "You must be ready to work for
Greece."

142   After the heroic death of her brother, Miss Haldin, a
character in *Under Western Eyes* by Joseph Conrad, says,
"Our dear one told me once to remember that men serve always something greater than themselves—the idea."

143   John Mason Brown said, "Existence is a strange bargain. Life owes little; we owe it everything. The only true
happiness comes from squandering ourselves for a purpose."

144   Father Theodore Hesburgh of Notre Dame said, "Patriotism is doing anything to serve one's country in whatever
way it needs most to be served at any given point in history."
So we serve our country by serving our community. And we
can serve our community today by . . .

145   John Stuart Mill said, "The man who has nothing to
do for his country cannot love it." And the man will do nothing for his community if he does not love his country or his
community. Love is service—love is helping out and giving a
hand.

146   In Jean Anouilh's play *Antigone* the citizen describes
real commitment: "To say yes, you have to sweat and roll
up your sleeves and plunge both hands into life up to the
elbows."

147   The British critic Cyril Connolly once said, "The civilized are those who get more out of life than the uncivilized, and for this the uncivilized have not forgiven them."

148   There's a great line in the play *Harvey* that fits here. Elwood P. Dowd is asked by Dr. Chumley, "God, man, haven't you any righteous indignation?"

149   Today the message set forth by Dr. King in his famous 1963 "Letter from Birmingham City Jail" is no less timely: "We must use time creatively and forever realize that the time is always ripe to do right. Now is the time to make real the promise of democracy, and transform our pending national elegy into a creative psalm of brotherhood. Now is the time to lift our national policy from the quicksand of racial injustice to the solid rock of human dignity."

150   One of the ways by which we may help ourselves and restore the legitimacy of authority of our schools and public confidence in them is to engage in self-renewal, not self-preservation. As John Gardner has said, "The tasks of renewal are endless. A society is being continually recreated, for good or ill, by its members. This will strike some as a burdensome responsibility, but it will summon others to greatness."

151   During these trying times I am reminded of what Edmund Burke wrote, "All that is necessary for the forces of evil to win in the world is for enough good men to do nothing."

152   Woodrow Wilson was the first college president to become President of the United States. He was thus a favorite to speak at college commencements. One of the first he gave was to Swarthmore. He asked the students something all of us should ask ourselves. "How many of you have devoted yourselves to the adventure? How many of you will volunteer to carry these spiritual messages of liberty to the world?"

153   An astute British commentator once described the uniqueness of the American way. In 1888 James Bryce, the diplomat and political philosopher, wrote: "Democracy has

not only taught the Americans how to use liberty without abusing it, and how to secure equality: it has also taught them fraternity. . . . There is still in the United States a sort of kindliness, a sense of human fellowship, a recognition of the duty of mutual help owed by man to man.

CIVIL-RIGHTS ADVOCATE

154   These words are from Romans, and they're from a man who was an itinerant preacher, a man who walked and rode and went by ship, and . . . yes, wrote letters, and kept them in boxes and books. I read to you from Paul's Letter to the Romans: "Let us not therefore judge one another any more: but judge this rather, that no man put a stumbling block or an occasion to fall in his brother's way."

155   In Periclean Athens, where democracy was born, someone asked the historian Thucydides, "Sir, when will justice come to Athens?" Thucydides replied, "Justice will not come to Athens until those who are not exploited are as indignant as those who are exploited."

156   When Jackie Robinson died his friend Jesse Jackson said in his eulogy, "He turned a stumbling block into a stepping stone." And so any obstacle can be a challenge. Today I would like to talk about two obstacles. . . .

157   Not long ago Bayard Ruskin made himself unpopular when he said, "The only power blacks have is when they share and join that power with whites." Yet it is obvious that when blacks fight against whites or whites against blacks, there can be no real solution to the difficulties and discriminations that sometimes divide us.

- We are a minority
- • We live in a democracy
- • • We must convince the majority to live up to democratic ideals

158   The French writer Albert Camus, at the time of Nazi Germany, wrote a letter to a German friend saying, "I should like to be able to love my country and still love justice."

159   I think Dr. Martin Luther King was right when he said, "The ultimate solution of the race problem lies in the willingness of men to obey the unenforceable."

160   As John Kennedy said about civil rights, "We are confronted primarily with a moral issue. It is as old as the Scriptures and is as clear as the American Constitution."

161   In his First Inaugural Address, Thomas Jefferson said, "All, too, will bear in mind this sacred principle, that though the will of the majority is in all cases to prevail; that will to be rightful must be reasonable; that the minority possess their equal rights, which equal law must protect, and to violate would be oppression."

162   In a sermon at the Riverside Church in New York City Dr. Ralph W. Sockman said, "Government laws are needed to give us civil rights, and God is needed to make us civil."

163   In 1968 Robert Kennedy said, "Each time a man stands up for an ideal or sets out to improve the lot of others, or strikes out against injustices, he sends forth a ripple of hope."

164   The Reverend Jesse Jackson once said, "I would challenge you today, all my brothers and sisters, to take the high road. Let nobody pull you down to the level of hate. Don't let the hatred get on the inside of you."

165   As the Civil War Negro leader Frederick Douglass asked, "Who will stand up for the downtrodden, open his mouth for the dumb and remember those in bonds, as if bound with them?"

166   In one of his last speeches, Martin Luther King spoke of a plot for a new novel found in the papers of an American novelist who had died recently. The plot dealt with a broken

and alienated family who inherited a big old mansion: The thrust of the novel was to turn on this theme: Can the alienated members of this family by being thrown together in the same house find reconciliation and regeneration in working out their common destiny?

167   Anatole France, the perceptive French writer knelt at the bier of Émile Zola, the towering French author who in the Dreyfus case evinced his commitment to fight injustice. France said, "He was a moment in the conscience of history."

168   William Lloyd Garrison spoke against the institution of slavery when it took courage to utter those convictions. Although warned by friends that his proposed newspaper the *Liberator* would arouse a storm of mob protest, he persisted in publishing it. The masthead of the first copy produced January 1, 1831 read: I am in earnest. I shall not excuse; I shall not equivocate; I shall not retreat a single inch; and I shall be heard.

CLUBMAN

169   Dr. Samuel Johnson once described to his friends at London's Cheshire Cheese an acquaintance he termed "a most unclubable man." Tonight we honor a "most clubable" man, who brightens the life of everyone he meets.

170   In Joseph Heller's novel *Something Happened* the main character, Robert Slocum, says, "I know at last what I want to be when I grow up. When I grow up I want to be a little boy."

171   Abraham Lincoln said, "It has ever been my experience that folks who have no vices have very few virtues."

172   As Mark Twain wrote, "There are few things harder to put up with than the annoyance of a good example." That is why my friend here annoys me so much.

173   To begin the party I would like to propose a toast in the words of Bobbie Burns, "Freedom and whisky gang together."

174   Winston Churchill had good advice about judging people, Never trust a man who has not a single redeeming vice. Fortunately our friend tonight is eminently worthy of trust. . . .

175   As James Thurber said, "We all have flaws and mine is being wicked."

COMMUNITY ARTS LEADER

176   Fortunately, we in America are a long way from the values of Nazi Germany, where Hermann Goering once said, "When I hear anyone talk of culture, I reach for my revolver." But there is some truth to the saying. Every time I hear anyone talk of culture, it means he's reaching for my pocketbook.

177   The composer Robert Schumann said to young musicians, "Love your instrument, but do not vainly suppose it is the only one." And, similarly, our community needs a rich and diversified resource of the arts—not only music, but museums, libraries, and even zoos.

178   Someone once asked the Duke of Windsor when he was the Prince of Wales, "What is your idea of civilization?" Edward answered, "It is a good idea. Why don't we start building it." Today we have the chance to help build civilization by contributing toward . . .

179   When the British General James Wolfe and his troops in 1759 rowed down the St. Lawrence River at night to surprise Montcalm and his French forces on the Plains of Abraham in Quebec, he recited aloud Gray's "Elegy in a Country Churchyard." When he uttered these words,

>   The boast of heraldry, the pomp of power,
>   And all that beauty, all that wealth e'er gave,

> Awaits like the inevitable hour:
> The paths of glory lead but to the grave,

he added "I'd rather be the poet who wrote these words than the general who conquered Quebec." And so it is the poets, musicians, and authors who grasp the inner truths of life.

180   Sir Thomas Beecham was once leading the symphony orchestra in a piece that called for an offstage trumpet to sound a long call. Beecham got to the point where the trumpet was to sound—but no trumpet. He paused, then went back a few bars and had the orchestra repeat the section leading to the point where the trumpet was to be heard. Once again, no trumpet. He threw down his baton and strode into the wings to see what had happened. There was his trumpeter in a tussle with a backstage guard, who was insisting. "You can't play that darn-fool trumpet in here—there's a concert going on!" Some of the needs of our symphony may seem strange and diverse.

181   It was Lewis Mumford who said, "A community whose life is not irrigated by art and science, by religion and philosophy, day upon day, is a community that exists only half alive." We do not want a city that is half dead—we want one that is alive and vibrant with artists as well as businessmen, musicians as well as lawyers, teachers as well as doctors.

182   There are those who question the sensitivity of the masses who visit our museums in greater numbers than they go to professional football games. In 1961, an abstract painting by Henri Matisse entitled "Le Bateau" was inadvertently hung upside down in the Museum of Modern Art in New York. The mistake went unnoticed for forty-seven days, during which time more than 100,000 people viewed the painting, apparently without noticing the error.

183   Michelangelo wrote, "My soul can find no staircase to Heaven unless it be through Earth's loveliness."

184   Anatole France once described a good critic as one "who narrates the adventures of his soul among masterpieces."

185   Pablo Picasso said, "When I was a child, my mother said to me, 'If you become a soldier, you'll be a general. If you become a priest you'll end up as Pope.' Instead, I became a painter and wound up as Picasso."

186   The French artist Paul Valéry described the creative eye this way, "To see is to forget the name of the thing one sees."

187   The Spanish painter Picasso once said, "When I was fourteen I knew I could draw like Michelangelo and I spent the rest of my life learning to draw like a child."

188   A friend once brought Picasso three paintings to sign. Picasso refused, declaring that all three were palpable fakes. "But," protested the exasperated friend, "I saw you paint these pictures with my own eyes." Picasso's unabashed answer was "I can paint fake Picassos just as well as anybody."

189   Picasso, with his feverish creativity and lavish talent, was a man of many styles, whose artistic life revealed a continuous process of exploration. "For me, a picture is neither an end nor an achievement but rather a lucky chance and art experience," he once said. "I try to represent what I have found, not what I am seeking. I do not seek—I find."

190   Peter Ustinov once said, "A thing of beauty is a profit forever."

191   Francis Ponge, one of France's finest modern poets, wrote of "the salutary lesson of smallness," the need to get close, to notice the texture of things. At the other end of the scale is the salutary lesson of largeness, which is just as vital, for it seems that most of us live in the middle sizes of life. We need all the grandeur we can get, as more and more people turn away from a disappointing society.

192   The late cellist Pablo Casals once said, "We are before anything men and we have to take part in the circumstances of

life. Who indeed should be more concerned than the artist with the defense of liberty and free inquiry, which are essential to his very creativity?"

193   "But what is civilized life?" asks Oswald in H. G. Wells's *Joan and Peter*. "Oh," replied Peter, "creative activities in an atmosphere of goodwill."

194   One of the greatest money raisers of his generation for civic institutions was Benjamin Franklin. He once gave this advice to a civic committee: "First, call upon all those who you know will give something: next apply to those you are uncertain whether they will give or not. Finally, visit those you are sure will give nothing, for in some of these you may be mistaken."

CONSUMER ADVOCATE

195   Attorney General Saxbe once said, "If businessmen insist on cutting corners and breaking laws in their quest for profits, they will set on a course that could wreck the entire free-enterprise system." Today I would like to talk on corporate law breaking.

- Price-fixing
- Political deal-making
- False advertising

196   Charles Dickens in *Martin Chuzzlewit* revealed the ways of businessmen: "Do other men, for they would do you." Businessmen must be more learned than I thought for many seem to follow that callous advice.

197   Doctor Samuel Johnson once wrote, "Promise, large promise is the soul of an advertisement." But today people are beginning to hold companies to their promises and claims. They are fed up with having their intelligence insulted and their pocketbook robbed. There are ways to strike back.

- Claims to watch out for
- • How to take action after purchase

198   Do you remember the lines of Emperor Jones in O'Neill's play: "For de little stealin' dey gits you in jail soon or late. For de big stealin' dey makes you emperor and puts you in de Hall o' Fame when you croaks"? Today I would like to talk about big stealing—stealing from the pockets of consumers.

199   Under Louis XI, King of France in 1481, there was an edict: "Anyone who sells butter containing stones or other things (to add to the weight) will be put into our pillory, then said butter will be placed on his head until entirely melted by the sun. Dogs may lick him and people offend him with whatever defamatory epithets they please without offense to God or King. If the sun is not warm enough, the accused will be exposed in the great hall of the gaol in front of a roaring fire, where everyone will see him."

200   The earliest prophet whose writings we may suppose ourselves to possess is Amos, the peasant poet. In 750 B.C. he saw and denounced the crimes of exploiters: "You men who crush the humble, and oppress the poor, only muttering, 'when will the new moon come, that we may sell our grain? When will the Sabbath be over, that we may sell our wheat?' Small you make your measures, large your weights. You cheat by tampering with the scales—and all to buy up innocent folk, to buy up the needy for a pair of sandals and to sell them the very refuse of your grain."

201   Many groups—consumerists, women's liberationists, legislators—are agitating for greater protection for women in the market place. It is my contention that the smartest purchasing agent in America is the American housewife.

202   The consumer advocate Ralph Nader said, "A 'whistle blower,' is anyone in any organization who has drawn a line in his own mind where responsibility to society transcends responsibility to the organization."

203   Four centuries before Christ the Athenian statesman Pericles said, "We must not say that a man who takes no interest in politics minds his own business: we say he has no business here at all."

CRITIC

204   Lewis Mumford once said, "The artist has a special task and duty; the task of reminding men of their humanity and the promise of their creativity." In this painting we unveil today we see the dream of man's potential and ability to express himself.

205   No critic better defined a work of art than George Jean Nathan, who said, "Art is the reaching out into the ugliness of the world for vagrant beauty and the imprisoning of it into a tangible dream."

206   The poet W. H. Auden said one criterion for good literature is pleasure. "Pleasure," he said, "is by no means an infallible guide, but it is the least fallible."

207   Justice Oliver Wendell Holmes once wrote this test for a good novel: "If after fifty pages you can't remember the color of the heroine's eyes, drop the book." By that test the book I am going to review today succeeds excellently. But there is a higher criterion beyond graphic description and high adventure.

208   Washington Irving once wrote, "The land of literature is a fancy land to those who view it at a distance, but like all other landscapes, the charm fades on a nearer approach, and the thorns and briars become visible."

209   The French critic André Gide once wrote, "It is with noble sentiments that the worst literature gets written."

210   August Strindberg said he saw the playwright as a lay preacher peddling the ideas of his time in popular form.

211   St. Augustine once said, "The world is a book—and those who do not travel read only one page."

212   The artist John Sargent once said that every time he painted a portrait he lost a friend.

DIPLOMAT

213   Talleyrand may have been one of the greatest French statesmen, but I disagree with the advice he once gave to young diplomats: "Above all, show no burning commitment." My colleague has always been imbued with the highest commitment to the service of his country.

214   Perhaps the oldest diplomat in literary history is Odysseus or Ulysses, whom Homer describes as "polymechanos"— fertile in plans or always coming up with new approaches or ways of accommodation. It is such ingenuity or resourcefulness that describes our honoree.

215   Napoleon once called ambassadors spies with a title. In that sense—although I never had a cloak and dagger—I do feel that an ambassador has the duty to report and assess the present situation.

216   Charles Dawes, after being Ambassador to the Court of St. James's, said, "Diplomatic life is easy on the brain but hell on the feet." Our speaker not only looks in good condition but his mind is that way too.

217   Too often State Department spokesmen seem to take the advice of French diplomat Baron Jacques Baeyens literally. When he was asked the role of a diplomatic spokesman, the French Foreign Office press chief said, "Mentir et dementir— lie and deny." Tonight I would like to talk frankly and then answer all questions about the state of détente.

218   In Greek mythology the patron god of diplomats was the tricky but charming Hermes. Hermes might have had this

distinction because he was also god of messengers and heralds. But the better reason is, I think, that he was known as the emissary between the upper and lower worlds or heaven and hell.

219   The social round of a diplomat is arduous if not impossible. I recall the case of Prince Wenzel Von Kaunitz-Rietberg, an eighteenth-century Austrian diplomat, who changed his clothes no fewer than thirty times daily. This obsession occupied about four hours a day.

220   King Charles II was said to be the perfect diplomat. He could tell you to go to hell in such a way that you actually looked forward to the place.

221   Adlai Stevenson once said the main ingredients of his life as an ambassador to the UN were protocol, alcohol, and Geritol. Well, I don't think red tape, red wine, and red tonic describes our speaker's life. It has been one of substantive work and negotiations.

222   In the seventeenth century, Sweden's Chancellor Count Oxenstierna, one of Europe's greatest statesmen, wrote to his son: "Thou dost not know, my son, with how little wisdom the world is governed?"

223   When Harold Macmillan was British Foreign Secretary he summed up his work: "A diplomat is forever poised between a cliché and an indiscretion." But from our speaker clichés we have never heard, and indiscretions we have never heard about.

224   It was Peter Ustinov who said, "A diplomat these days is nothing but a head-waiter who's allowed to sit down occasionally." And I confess in the last few weeks I have had little chance to sit down. I have traveled to . . .

225   Former UN Ambassador Charles Yost once said, "Show me a man with both feet on the ground and I'll show you a man who can't get his pants on." Diplomats like architects must have vision—an ideal on which to construct world order.

226   In 1960 Prime Minister Harold Macmillan's speech to the UN was interrupted when Soviet Premier Nikita Khrushchev took off his shoe and pounded on the table with it. In the best tradition of British unflappability Macmillan remarked, "I'd like that translated, if I may." Today we should try to interpret some recent developments in foreign policy.

227   There is a saying in the British Foreign Service about payment for overwork: "You'll get it in heaven, if you get there." And I am sure that if our speaker gets there he will find ample reward, because his services and contributions to his country have been many.

228   Buckminster Fuller once observed that there were 100 million people in India who had never heard the words "America" or "United States."

229   I recall what Napoleon once said to an envoy, "Go, sir, and gallop and don't forget that the world was made in six days. You can ask me for anything except time."

230   What British Foreign Secretary Lord John Russell said 125 years ago is timely today, "If peace cannot be maintained with honor, it is no longer peace."

231   As UN Secretary-General Trygve Lie once described it, "We are now entering a period best characterized as a cold peace."

232   Former British Ambassador to the United States, Sir Harold Caccia once said, "Man is a peculiar animal. He seems only to be able to read the handwriting on the wall when his back is up to it."

233   In 1888 President-elect Benjamin Harrison said, "We Americans have no commission from God to police the world."

234   When I consider some of the recent actions of the United Nations, I recall a memoir of Robert Kennedy by Jack Newfield. Kennedy is described walking to his fourteenth-floor window in New York City and looking down at the tugs and

barges slicing through the East River. From his Manhattan apartment, he saw a boat sailing out. "Look at that!" he exclaimed. "There's a ship called *World Justice,* and it is moving away from the United Nations."

235   "Politics," wrote John Kenneth Galbraith, "is not the art of the possible. It consists in choosing between the disastrous and the unpalatable."

236   The favorite policy motto of British Prime Minister Herbert Asquith was "Wait and See."

237   Will Rogers said, "The United States has never lost a war or won a conference."

238   There is a Spanish proverb "En boca cerrada no entran moscas—If you keep your mouth shut, the flies won't get in."

239   Speaking at Princeton University in 1954, former Ambassador George F. Kennan warned: "If there is any great lesson we Americans need to learn . . . it is that we must be gardeners and not mechanics in our approach to world affairs. . . . We can afford to be patient, and even occasionally suffer reverses, placing our confidence in the longer and deeper workings of history."

240   The suddenly-famous Watergate complex, with its prestigious apartments, offices, and a shop by Yves St. Laurent, is no gift. But the bronze figure of Benito Juárez in front of the complex is—from the Mexican government. Juárez, the Mexican President, who once studied for the priesthood, devoted his life to dissolving feudalism and was the prominent political figure in Mexico from 1856 to 1872. The inscription on his statue reads: "The best respect for others is peace."

241   Adlai Stevenson perhaps best explained the difference between a general and a diplomat. "Our goal," he said, "is not just to win the cold *war* but to persuade the cold *world.*"

242   Former King Edward, the Duke of Windsor, gave this good advice about adapting to protocol. "Only two rules really

count: Never miss an opportunity to relieve yourself; never miss a chance to sit down and rest your feet."

243 The best definition of diplomacy is this: the art of jumping into trouble without making a splash.

244 I'd like to think that an international crisis is like sex— as long as you keep talking about it, nothing happens.

245 Alexander Woollcott once described a diplomat as a babe in a silk hat playing with dynamite.

246 Sir Harold Caccia, while British Ambassador in Washington, once said, "If you are to stand up for your government, you must be able to stand up *to* your government.

247 It was Averell Harriman who observed that summit meetings or high-level conferences are always courteous and polite. Name calling is left to foreign ministers and ambassadors.

248 In *Pudd'nhead Wilson* Mark Twain offered sage advice for the success of a diplomat: "In statesmanship get the formalities right, never mind about the moralities." In that case I want to be sure that the program starts in the right way.

249 Back in the first century Plutarch warned that statesmen are not only liable to give account of what they say or do in public, but there is a busy inquiry made into their very meals, beds, marriages, every other sportive or serious action.

250 When Woodrow Wilson was pleading the cause of the League of Nations in 1920, he said, "My clients are the children; my clients are the next generation." It is for our children, for peace in our children's world, that we plead in this campaign.

DOCTOR

251 In *The Magic Mountain*, Thomas Mann wrote: "All interest in disease and death is only another expression of interest in life."

252 Twenty years ago Bernard Baruch testified to a White House committee, "There are no such things as incurables, there are only things for which man has not found a cure."

253 Today a hospital bed is like a parked taxi with the meter ticking not nickels but dollars.

254 Not long ago a corporation executive came into a doctor's office in Philadelphia for a checkup. He showed signs of overwork and stress. He was warned to slow down, to take up a hobby—perhaps painting—to relax. He readily agreed and left the office. The next day the executive phoned and announced enthusiastically, "Doc, this painting is wonderful. I've already done ten."

255 Doctor William Mayo of the Mayo Clinic said a specialist is one who knows more and more about less and less.

256 Dean Swift observed that the best doctors were Doctor Diet, Doctor Quiet, and Doctor Merriman.

ECONOMIST

257 Ever since the time of Thomas Carlyle, our profession of economics has been called "the dismal science." And I suppose one reason people think it "dismal" is that we are mostly predicting bad news. Well, the news I have today is not all bad.

258 George Bernard Shaw once said of our profession, "If all economists were laid end to end, they would not reach a conclusion." Well, Shaw notwithstanding, I would like to draw a tentative conclusion about the health of our economy today.

259 As Harry Truman said, "It's a recession when your neighbor loses his job; it's a depression when you lose yours." And in line with that definition, I would like to talk about those sectors of the economy that are strong and those that are soft.

- Soft—housing, steel, autos, etc.
- Strong—plastics, computerware, etc.

260   Dr. Elly Staegnel, who was a student in Munich in the 1920s, told how in the inflation-rocked Weimar republic it took a whole month's salary to buy the paper to write her doctoral thesis. It was a billion marks for a street-car ride; to drink a glass of milk, you pulled down the shades so no one would see you had milk. With the current double-digit inflation, we may be approaching that point. The question is, What steps can government take to arrest this bloating of our economy?

261   In 594 B.C. when sheep and a bushel of grain rose to a drachma in Athens, the legislator Solon enacted a law limiting women to three garments. Today the increase in taxes or the cutting of government programs has the same effect.

262   Inflation is almost as old as man's written records. The Babylonian Code of Hammurabi (*circa* 2000 B.C.), which was the world's first known detailed system of law, contained regulations on payments and measures for grain and other products that added up to a form of price control. Ever since that time there has been debate about controls or no controls—the state-regulated or free economy.

263   Did you know that the expression "stone broke" originated from the old custom of breaking a craftsman's stone bench when he failed to pay his debts?

264   Marco Polo told of how in ancient China the emperors began to issue paper money. One of the great ministers became wealthy by this scheme. But it soon came about you could scarcely buy a bowl of rice for ten thousand bills. By government deficit spending, we are also issuing paper. It is not altogether impossible for us to have in sight the day when like Weimar Germany we will use wheelbarrows for pocketbooks.

265   In the eighteenth century, Edmund Burke warned, "The age of chivalry is gone; that of sophisters, economists and calculators has succeeded." Well, as an economist I have to be

a calculator and those economic predictions have often been called sophistry—or incomprehensible data. Today let me talk about some economic facts of life we all understand.

266   Washington tells us the economy is sound. That may be true but the sound is a little mournful—a little doleful. That is because although they try to put a good face on the facts the statistics indicated a stalled economy. Let us examine some of those statistics.

267   "If the nation's economists were laid end to end, they would still point in all directions."

268   Politicians and wives agree on one thing—if you postpone payment until sometime in the future, it's not really spending.

269   Inflation might be called prosperity with high blood pressure.

270   An economist is one who states the obvious in terms of the incomprehensible.

271   Three hundred years ago a Frenchman, Jean Baptiste Colbert, Louis XIV's Minister of Finance, is supposed to have said that "the art of taxation consists in so plucking the goose as to obtain the largest amount of feathers with the least possible amount of hissing."

272   Calvin Coolidge remarked, "I am for economy. After that, I am for more economy."

273   I am reminded today of the words of Cicero: "Men do not realize how great a revenue economy is."

274   The historian Carl Becker used to quote the old lady's comment on the Great Depression: "What a pity this old depression had to come along just when times are so bad."

275   The well-known economist John Kenneth Galbraith once remarked: "Pessimism in our time is infinitely more respectable than optimism: the man who foresees peace, prosper-

ity, and a decline in juvenile delinquency is a negligent and vacuous fellow. The man who foresees catastrophe has a gift of insight which insures that he will become a radio commentator, an editor of *Time* or go to Congress."

276   Alben W. Barkley once described an economist as "a guy with a Phi Beta Kappa key on one end of his watch chain and no watch on the other end."

277   With our problems on inflation I am reminded of the words of Ernest Hemingway, "The first panacea for a mismanaged nation is inflation of the currency; the second is war. Both bring a temporary prosperity; both bring a permanent ruin. But both are the refuge of political and economic opportunists."

278   In his budget message of 1972 Richard Nixon said, "The budget is a superb deflator of rhetoric."

279   Franklin Delano Roosevelt once noted: "Any government, like any family, can occasionally spend a little more than it earns. But you and I know that continuance of that habit means the poorhouse."

280   Daniel Webster once reacted to a Jacksonian bank bill by slamming down his first against his Senate desk, and as the blood trickled down his fingers, he said, "If this bill passes, charity will have to lend a mantle to wrap the pale corpse of a nation's credit."

EDUCATOR

281   Finley Peter Dunne, in his *Colleges and Degrees* wrote: "D'ye think th' colledges has much to do with th' progress iv the wurruld?" asked Mr. Hennessy. "D'ye think," said Mr. Dooley, " 'tis th' mill that makes th' water run?"

282   Milton Eisenhower said, "It does not necessarily follow that a scholar in the humanities is also a humanist—but it

should. For what does it avail a man to be the greatest expert on John Donne if he cannot hear the bell tolling?"

283   In *The Male Animal* by James Thurber and Elliott Nugent, Ed says, "I believe that a college should be concerned with ideas. Not just your ideas . . . or my ideas, but all ideas. . . . I have been putting ideas into young people's heads for forty-two years with no—visible—results whatever."

284   Thomas Wolfe wrote, "Knowledge . . . is finding out something for oneself with pain, with joy, with exultancy, with labor, and with all the little ticking, breathing moments of our lives, until it is ours as that only is ours which is rooted in the structure of our lives. Knowledge is a potent and subtle distillation of experience, a rare liquor, and it belongs to the person who has the power to see, think, feel, taste, smell, and observe for himself, and who has hunger for it."

285   A person once sarcastically asked Robert M. Hutchins, former president of the University of Chicago, if communism was still being taught at the university. "Yes," replied Dr. Hutchins, "and cancer at the medical school." Hutchins realized you can't take the "liberal" out of "liberal arts"—the scope should be broad not restricted.

286   Dean Inge said the aim of education is the knowledge not of facts but of values. So what are the values students should learn?

287   Aristotle was once asked how much better off educated men were than uneducated men. "As much," said Aristotle, "as the living are to the dead."

288   Clark Kerr as president of the University of California once summed up the major problems of college education—sex for students, athletics for alumni, and parking for faculty.

289   We may remember what President Garfield's idea of university education was—the student on one end of a bench and a professor like Mark Hopkins of Williams College on the

other. But the point is valid—the relationship of professor to student is the core of university life.

290   Dr. Samuel Johnson wrote that "no man but a blockhead ever wrote except for money."

291   The great educator Horace Mann closed his career as president of Antioch College the day before he died. He gave a commencement address which ended: "Be ashamed to die until you have won some victory for humanity."

292   The best advice an educator can get is what Dr. James Conant once told Nathan Pusey, who succeeded him. "You have two choices before you: you can either get the job done or get the credit for doing it. You can't do both." He was quoting the warning of Columbia President Nicholas Murray Butler.

293   Former president of Harvard James Conant said, "Behold the turtle. He makes progress only when he sticks his neck out!" In university education we can no longer afford to play safe.

294   Adlai Stevenson said, "The university is the archive of the Western ideal, the keeper of the Western culture, the guardian of our heritage, the dwelling place of the free mind, the teacher of teachers."

295   In the sixteenth century Queen Elizabeth noted the presence of her privy councillor, Sir Walter Mildmay, who had been missing from court for some time. "Sir Walter," she said, "where have you been?" Mildmay, who had been away establishing Emmanuel College at Cambridge, replied, "Madam, I have been away planting an acorn. And when it becomes an oak, God only knoweth what it will amount to." Today we are going to plant some acorns.

296   Woodrow Wilson said, "The purpose of a university is to make young gentlemen as unlike their fathers as possible."

297   Adlai Stevenson once said, "We must reserve the element of quality in our traditional pursuit of equality. We must

not, in opening schools to everyone, confuse the idea that all should have equal chances with the notion that all have equal endowments."

298   In one of the most famous incidents in the Bible, the Lord summoned Moses to the top of Mount Sinai. There he appeared to Moses in the form of a fiery cloud, and there, to the accompaniment of thunder and lightning, he presented Moses with the Ten Commandments. That, as far as I know, is the earliest use of audiovisual techniques for mass education.

299   Robert Hutchins, president of the University of Chicago, said, "The object of education is to prepare the young to educate themselves throughout their lives."

300   The philosopher Dr. Alfred North Whitehead once wrote, "Education is discipline for the adventure of life."

301   Educator John Dewey has been much misunderstood. Listen to what he said about discipline: "Discipline is positive. Discipline means power at command: mastery of the resources available for carrying through the actions undertaken."

302   As H. G. Wells wrote, "Human history becomes more and more a race between education and catastrophe."

303   The philosopher Jacques Barzun wrote this criterion of education, "The test and the use of man's education is that he finds pleasure in the exercise of his mind."

304   I like Robert Frost's concept of the educator: "to rumple their brains as you might rumple their hair."

305   I remember from history classes the French student François Quesnay who had to walk from his home to Paris to beg books—in a period of eighteen years while studying to be a physician he walked fifty thousand miles.

306   The record of educators has not been one of unmixed success—sometimes potential geniuses are overlooked. Yeats and Shaw were failed as poor spellers. Franklin and Picasso

were flunked in math. Poe, Shelley, and Whistler were expelled from school. Edison was at the bottom of the class. Watt was called "dull and inept." Einstein was said to be mentally retarded.

307   Dr. Alfred North Whitehead said, "Celibacy does not suit a university; it must mate itself with action."

308   When President Lowell of Harvard was asked what it takes to make a university great, he answered, "Three hundred years."

309   Once when discussing education the English essayist Joseph Addison said, "Education is a companion which no misfortune can depress, no crime can alienate, no despotism can enslave. At home a friend, abroad an introduction, in solitude a solace, and in society an ornament. It chastens vice, it guides virtue, it gives, at once, grace and government to genius. Without it, what is man? A splendid slave, a reasoning savage."

310   John Kennedy once remarked that "the human mind is our fundamental resource."

311   One of the wittiest books in 1970 bore the title *Due to a Lack of Interest, Tomorrow Has Been Canceled.* The author, Irene Kampen took her title from a notice she saw on a college bulletin board.

ENGINEER

312   Dr. Karl Kapp of Basel University in Switzerland, addressing an international conference on the quality of life, said, "Had there been a computer in 1872 it would have predicted that by now there would have been so many horse-drawn vehicles, it would be impossible to clear up all the manure."

313   Winston Churchill said, "We want engineers in this world but not a world of engineers."

314   In the *Adventure of the Dancing Men*, Sherlock Holmes says, "What one man can invent another can discover."

315   Lewis Mumford has written: "What is the function of transportation? What place does locomotion occupy in the whole spectrum of human needs? Perhaps the first step in developing an adequate transportation policy would be to clear our minds of technocratic cant. Those who believe that transportation is the chief end of life should be put in orbit at a safe lunar distance from the earth. The prime purpose of passenger transportation is not to increase the amount of physical movement but to increase the possibilities for human association, cooperation, personal intercourse, and choice."

316   South of Pittsburgh, Pennsylvania, in the rural section of Colliers Township, a bridge was being built on Interstate Highway 79. It was to span a six-hundred foot chasm. The ramps on each end of the bridge were completed, and the bridge was almost finished when they discovered that it was thirteen feet out of alignment. It didn't connect. Remember, men, the road we are on is only one section of an endless highway. Be sure that it is lined up with the other stretch.

317   In 1829 an official in the U.S. Patent Office resigned because, as he said, "Everything important has already been invented."

318   Automation is not new. About the first century A.D. Hero of Alexandria invented the aeolipile, a turbine engine to open the doors in an Egyptian temple. Hero thus was the father of automation.

319   As Sir Isaac Newton said, "To every action there is always opposed an equal reaction."

ENVIRONMENTALIST

320   Some of you may have heard this recipe for "Preserved Children": "Take 1 large field; ½ dozen children; 2 or 3 small

dogs; a pinch of brook and pine. Mix children and dogs well together, stirring constantly. Pour the brook over the pebbles, sprinkle the field with flowers, spread over a deep blue sky and bake in sun. When brown, put away in cool tub." And when we think of the ingredients in this recipe, we wonder what we are doing to preserve those ingredients—the parks, the clean streams, unpolluted air. . . .

321 In the eighteenth century, the poet Oliver Goldsmith warned of threats to the environment with these lines:

Ill fares the land, to hastening ills a prey,
Where wealth accumulates, and men decay.

322 When the astronaut James Lovell received the Presidential Medal of Freedom, he spoke of the loneliness and sterility of space. He remembered seeing our planet in the distance with its color of life, and then he realized that "Earth was the only place we had to go." And yet we continue to burn up its energy and waste its resources.

323 In Lewis Carroll's *Through the Looking-Glass*, the White Queen says to Alice, "What's one and one and one and one and one and one and one and one and one and one?" And Alice replied: "I don't know. I lost count." And it is evident that in the population race we aren't keeping count.

324 The historian and philosopher Arnold Toynbee said about overpopulation: "We have been God-like in our planned breeding of our domesticated plants and animals, but we have been rabbit-like in our unplanned breeding of ourselves."

325 The last speech Adlai Stevenson ever gave was to the United Nations in July, 1965, a few days before his death. "We travel together," he said, "passengers on a little spaceship, dependent on its vulnerable reserves of air and soil: all committed for our safety to its security and peace: preserved from annihilation only by the care, the work and, I will say, the life we give our fragile craft."

326   In the early nineteenth century, when the U.S. government was pressuring Indian tribes to leave the Midwestern territories, one official approached Tecumseh, the great warrior chief, who replied: "Sell the country! Why not sell the air, the clouds, the great sea?" Well, we did exploit the air and sea for commercial use and today we must pay the price for reclamation.

327   Henry David Thoreau once wrote, "The frontiers are not east or west, north or south but wherever a man fronts a fact."

328   In Thornton Wilder's play *Our Town* the young lady who died comes back to relive a day in her life. She says, "Oh, earth, you're too wonderful for anybody to realize you! Do any human beings ever realize life while they live it?"

329   Theodore Roosevelt was one of the first conservationists. He said, "I recognize the right and duty of this generation to develop and use our natural resources, but I do not recognize the right to waste them, or to rob by wasteful use the generations that come after us."

330   In *The Outermost House,* Henry Beston writes, "Do no dishonour to the earth lest you dishonour the spirit of man."

331   Today we are witnessing what Stewart Udall described in *The Quiet Crisis,* "America today stands poised on a pinnacle of wealth and power, yet we live in a land of vanishing beauty, of increasing ugliness, of shrinking open space, and of an overall environment that is diminished daily by pollution and noise and blight."

332   Dante wrote, "Nature is the art of God."

EULOGIST

333   I console myself with these words from the British poet Thomas Campbell, "To live in hearts we leave behind is not to die." The memory of our friend will not die.

- The community will remember him for
-- His colleagues will remember him for
--- His family will remember him for

334   I would like to close with these words from Matthew Arnold:

> My special thanks, whose even-balanced soul,
> From first youth tested up to extreme old age,
> Business could not make dull, nor passion wild:
> Who saw life steadily and saw it whole.

335   The words most appropriate this time are Shakespeare's,

> His life was gentle, and the elements
> So mix'd in him that Nature might stand up
> And say to all the world, "This was a man!"

336   When singer Maurice Chevalier died in 1971, his writer friend Alan Jay Lerner wrote, "I envy the angels."

337   Before the First World War the mistress of a literary salon asked a young journalist, "What do you love?" And the young Walter Lippmann replied, "The living world."

338   Learned Hand once said, "A man's life, like a piece of tapestry, is made up of many strands which interwoven make a pattern."

- The strand as leader in his profession
-- as community leader
--- as parent and husband

339   In *As You Like It*, Shakespeare writes:

> O good old man, how well in thee appears
> The constant service of the antique world,
> When service sweat for duty, not for meed!"

340   I am reminded today of what Samuel Butler wrote in *The Way of All Flesh*, "Every man's work, whether it be literature or music or pictures or architecture or anything else, is always a portrait of himself."

341   As the poet Ariosto once said, "Nature made him and then broke the mould."

342   In an address at Amherst College John F. Kennedy said, "A nation reveals itself not only by the men it produces but also by the men it honors, the men it remembers."

343   The former governor of Puerto Rico, Muñoz Marin, was often called the father of that American Commonwealth. But that statesman in his biography clearly attributes his success to the inspiration of his father, who for so many years championed the cause of Puerto Rico's self-determination. At his death the young Muñoz wrote a poignant poem with the ending lines, "I would be a giant to embrace the mountains he contemplated in his boyhood."

344   At the pass of Thermopylae a band of twenty Greeks led by Leonidas withstood thousands of Persians in 480 B.C. On the rocks the poet Simonides had carved these words commemorating that valiant fight: "Go, passer-by, and to Sparta tell that we in faithful public service fell."

345   When Theodore Roosevelt learned of the death of his son Quentin, on July 14, 1916, he penned a noble letter including these lines: "Only those are fit to live who do not fear to die and none are fit to die who have shrunk from the joy of life. Both life and death are parts of the same great adventure worthily carried through by the man who puts his personal safety first. . . . Pride is the portion only of those who know bitter sorrow or the foreboding of bitter sorrow. But all of us who gave service, and stand ready for service, are torchbearers. We run with the torches until we fall."

EXECUTIVE

346   Woodrow Wilson said that every new President would like to write his own record from the start on a blank sheet of paper. But he cannot—he must begin by writing between the lines of what past Presidents have written.

347   John Kennedy said the day before he was elected, "The chief duty of the President is to put before the public 'the unfinished business' of our time."

348   General Eisenhower once described leadership as "the ability to decide what is to be done and then to get others to want to do it."

349   In *Rabbit, Run* by John Updike, I remember the old gas-station attendant giving this advice to the restless man called Rabbit, "The only way to get somewhere, you know, is to figure out where you're going before you go there."

350   Dean Acheson used to quote General Marshall's warning: "Don't fight the problem; decide it."

351   When two men in our organization always agree, one of them is unnecessary.

352   A committee is too often a group that keeps minutes and loses hours.

353   Herbert Bayard Swope once said, "I cannot give you the formula for success but I can give you the formula for failure —which is, Try to please everybody."

354   Abraham Lincoln once said, "The occasion is piled high with difficulty, and we must rise with the occasion. As our case is new, so we must think anew and act anew. We must disenthrall ourselves."

355   Herbert Hoover appointed a commission in 1929 to plot the United States's course through 1952. They studied and studied, and planned and planned. They had five hundred researchers working. They produced thirteen volumes. They had a sixteen-hundred-page summary that didn't contain one word about atomic energy, jet propulsion, the wonder drugs called antibiotics, or transistors.

356   In her book *Spring Harvest,* Gladys Taber writes, "Problems are universal. It's facing them that is individual."

357   The problem we face suggests a reply by Dr. Chaim Weizmann of Israel to President Harry Truman. President Truman in a talk with the new Israeli President in Washington said, "Have you ever considered what it would be like to be President of 140 million?" Dr. Weizmann replied, "Have you ever considered, Mr. President, what it would be like to be President of half a million little presidents?"

358   On paper the plan sounds good but I doubt its practicality. It reminds me of the play *Rainmaker,* where Starbuck, a swaggering adventurer, says, "Nothing is ever as good when I get it in my hand as when I had it in my head."

359   In Edna Ferber's *So Big,* the young girl Maartje says, "You can't run away far enough. Except you stop living you can't run away from life."

360   In a letter to Theodore Roosevelt during the 1902 coal strike Henry Cabot Lodge wrote, "Isn't there something we can appear to be doing?"

361   As Sherlock Holmes told Dr. Watson as they pondered the case of the Red-Headed League, "It is quite a three-pipe problem."

362   At a speech to the Phi Beta Kappa chapter at Harvard Ralph Waldo Emerson cited to them the story of the "old oracle [who] said, 'All things have two handles: beware of the wrong one.' "

363   An assistant rushed into the office of management wizard William Knudsen one day, very upset because a certain report was missing. How could they act? "There are two kinds of reports," Knudsen said calmly. "One says you can't do it. The other says it has been done. The first kind is no good. The second kind you don't need."

364   Harry Truman put it in a wonderful way when he said, "The President hears a hundred voices telling him that he is

the greatest man in the world. He must listen carefully indeed to hear the one voice that tells him he is not."

365   To close I would like to quote an old Chinese proverb: "That the birds of worry and care fly above your head, this you cannot change. But that they build nests in your hair—this you can prevent."

366   In April, 1861, the newly inducted President Lincoln took office as Southern states, one by one, declared their separation from the Union. To his loyal supporter Governor Andrew Curtin of Pennsylvania he wired this terse message. The telegram was read to Governor Curtin in Harrisburg in the measured decisive tones of the clerk. "I think the necessity of being ready increases. Look to it."

EXPLORER

367   When Commander Neil Armstrong was invited to address the joint session of Congress after his moon trip, he told them, "Man must understand his universe in order to understand his destiny."

368   Willa Cather wrote, "A pioneer should have imagination, should be able to enjoy the idea of things more than the things themselves."

369   In the early seventeenth century Captain John Smith wrote in his diary, "These are the times for men to live—to spread your wings and soar like an eagle."

370   When Captain James Cook, the eighteenth-century English explorer of the Pacific, was asked why he felt the call to explore, he said, "I had not the ambition only to go farther than any other man, but as far as man can go."

371   On January 9, 1969, Astronaut Commander Frank Borman and his two missile mates were welcomed by an invitation to speak to a joint session of Congress. He spoke

of their recent Christmas Eve flight and their nearer sight of the moon.

Quoting Archibald MacLeish's poem, he said that a space flight reminds one that we are "all riders on the earth" together and that exploration is stirred by brotherhood. His one phrase at the close of the speech epitomized that sense of humanity in space adventure. "Exploration is really the essence of the human spirit."

FARM LEADER

372   As Pope John XXIII said, "People go to ruin in three ways—women, gambling, and farming. My family chose the slowest."

373   In the *Congressional Record* there was an item printed some years ago:

> Some people tell us there ain't no hell
> But they never farmed, so how can they tell.

374   Farming looks nice—from a car window.

FASHION DESIGNER

375   I like what Oscar Wilde wrote: "Fashion is that by which the fantastic becomes, for a moment, universal."

376   Shakespeare penned this criticism of our profession: "Fashion wears out more apparel than the man." Yet shouldn't our goal be to create the timeless article?

377   The English essayist William Hazlitt said, "Fashion is gentility running away from vulgarity and afraid of being overtaken."

378   When the impeccable Fred Astaire picked up his suit from his tailor John Galupo, he crumpled it up and threw it against the wall, saying every suit needs to look worn.

• Clothes should be durable
•• should look comfortable
••• should look part of you

379   To some extent, Queen Marie of Rumania was right: "Just like etiquette is for people with no breeding, fashions exist for women with no taste."

380   As George Bernard Shaw said, "A fashion is nothing but an induced epidemic."

381   As Alfred Hitchcock once said about movies, "Self-plagiarism is style."

FATHER

382   Theodore Roosevelt once stopped short a cabinet meeting, to keep a date he had to play with his sons, by saying, "I have learned many years ago you can never keep children waiting."

383   I am aware of what Oscar Wilde wrote about fatherhood: "Fathers should be neither seen nor heard. That is the only proper basis for family life." So with that advice I will be appropriately brief.

384   In the Bible's Proverbs, King Solomon wrote: "A wise son maketh a glad father." And similarly I might add a wise son-in-law makes a happy father-in-law. I am happy for my daughter . . .

385   I feel somewhat like Themistocles, who pointed to his new baby and said, "He governs Greece because he governs his mother, his mother governs me, and I govern the Athenians and the Athenians govern Greece." Now I am not saying my new grandson runs the company but . . .

386   Sophocles in his play *Antigone* wrote: "What greater ornament to a son than a father's glory or to a father than a son's honorable conduct?"

387   As a father I am often reminded of the words of Theodore Roosevelt: "I can govern the United States or I can govern my daughter Alice, but I can't do both."

388   On this proud occasion I am reminded of the Persian proverb "Children are a bridge to heaven."

389   There is a Chinese proverb which reads: "Govern a family as you would cook a small fish—very gently."

390   As a father I have often pondered the question posed by author Catherine Drinker Bowen in her book *Family Portrait:* "Does fate lie in the seed, or does one's future depend upon the ground where the seed falls?"

FEMINIST

391   The perceptive French critic Alexis de Tocqueville wrote about America 140 years ago: "If I were asked . . . to what the singular prosperity and groving strength of that people ought mainly to be attributed, I should reply: To the superiority of their women." Certainly De Tocqueville could be describing the excellence and superiority of this group today.

392   In Henrik Ibsen's *A Doll's House* Nora reacts to her husband's demand that she had a sacred duty to be wife and mother. Nora replies: "First and foremost my duty is to myself." So today we must examine our own priority of needs as women.

393   On a recent television program a man was asked to list all the qualities he wanted in a wife. He said, Someone to cook, buy the food, clean the house, raise the family, wash the dishes, mend the clothes, do the laundry, keep household accounts, run errands, and be full of cheer and comfort. At that point a woman on the panel piped up, "I want a wife too." Of course, all of us would want a girl Friday at home as well as the office, but what do we lose in our own identity when we try to play all these roles instead of being ourselves?

394   One of the first advocates of woman's rights was Abigail Adams. She once said, "We have too many high-sounding words and too few actions that correspond with them." And today too many of us use "women's lib" as an excuse for our shortcomings and don't seize on what opportunities we have in the way of educational training, career jobs . . .

395   In the British play *The Chalk Garden,* the grandmother asks the teacher, "Who are you?" She replies, "A woman who has lost touch with unessential things." Today I would like to talk about the essential things in our lives as women.

> • Our homes
> •• Our families
> ••• Ourselves

396   Perhaps the first voice raised in America on behalf of women was Abigail Adams, who wrote to her husband, John, at the time of the adoption of the Declaration of Independence: "I long to hear that you have declared an independence—and by the way in this new code of law I desire you would remember the ladies." Well, our Founding Fathers did not remember the ladies. In terms of suffrage, property, and other legal rights we were quite limited. But the ERA—Equal Rights Amendment—will be passed soon and today I would like to sketch for you some of the new opportunities that will be flowing from that ratified amendment.

397   I feel it appropriate today to recall what William Allen White said, "My advice to the women's clubs of America is to raise more hell and fewer dahlias."

FOUNDER

398   In the Old Testament it is written that "the stone which the builders refused is become the head stone of the corner."

399   Woodrow Wilson in his Inaugural Address said, "This is not a day of triumph; it is a day of dedication. Here muster, not the forces of party, but the forces of humanity. Men's hearts wait upon us; men's lives hang in the balance; men's hopes call upon us to say what we will do."

400   In Tennessee Williams' *A Streetcar Named Desire*, Blanche says, "Maybe we are a long way from being made in God's image, but . . . there has been some progress. . . . Such things as art—as poetry and music—such kinds of new light have come into the world. . . . In some kinds of people some tenderer feelings have had some little beginning! That we have got to make grow! And cling to, and hold as our flag! In this dark march toward whatever brutes!"

401   In *Joan of Lorraine* by Maxwell Anderson the character Mary says: "I have studied [Joan of Arc] and read about her all my life. She has a meaning for me—She means that the great things in this world are all brought about by faith—that all the leaders who count are dreamers and people who see visions. The realists and common-sense people can never begin anything. They can only do what the visionaries plan for them."

402   In the play *Harvey* by Mary Chase one of the characters says, "The difference between a fine oil painting and a mechanical thing like a photograph is simply this: a photograph shows only the reality; a painting shows not only the reality but the dream behind it. It's our dreams that keep us going. That separate us from the beasts. I wouldn't even want to live if I thought it was all just eating and sleeping."

403   Mary Webb in her novel *Precious Bane* writes, "Saddle your dreams afore you ride 'em."

404   In Ellen Glasgow's novel *Vein of Iron*, Ada is determined to rehabilitate the old family home. "She had a sense, more a feeling than a vision, of the dead generations behind her. They had come to life there in the past; they were lending her their fortitude; they were reaching out to her in adversity.

This was the heritage they had left. She could lean back on their strength; she could recover that lost certainty of a continuing tradition." "It will be starting over from the very bottom," Ralph said. "Well, we're at the bottom, so it's high time for us to start."... "You're a dreamer, Ada. It's queer that a dreamer should be a rock to lean on."

405   It is written in Isaiah, "Behold, I lay in Zion for a foundation a stone, a tried stone, a precious corner stone, a sure foundation."

FRIEND

406   In *Orange Shroud for the Lady,* J. D. MacDonald describes the difference between an acquaintance and a friend: "The dividing line is communication, I think. A friend is someone to whom you can say any jackass thing that enters your mind. With acquaintances, you are forever aware of their slightly unreal image of you, and to keep them content, you edit yourself to fit. Many marriages are between acquaintances. You can be with a person for three hours of your life and have a friend. Another one will remain an acquaintance for thirty years."

407   The poet William Butler Yeats wrote:

> Count where man's glory begins and ends
> And say my glory was I had such friends.

408   In the last letter received by President Andrew Jackson from his mother she wrote: "In this world you will have to make your own way. To do that you must have friends. You can make friends by being honest, and you can keep them by being steadfast. You must keep in mind that friends worth having will in the long run expect as much from you as they give to you. To forget an obligation or be ungrateful for a kindness is a base crime—not merely a fault or a sin but an actual crime."

409   I recall the first time we met. It was as Winston Churchill said of Franklin Delano Roosevelt: "Meeting him was like opening a bottle of champagne."

410   In Lloyd C. Douglas's *Doctor Hudson's Secret Journal*, Dr. Hudson discovered that "to lose a friend in whom one had invested something of one's personality was to have lost a certain amount of one's self."

411   Harry Emerson Fosdick once observed, "No man is the whole of himself; his friends are the rest of him."

412   Robert Louis Stevenson said, "A friend is a present you give yourself."

413   Ralph Waldo Emerson once said a friend is one with whom you can think aloud—so if I may let myself think aloud with my closest friends . . .

FUND RAISER

414   Someone asked Arnold Toynbee to boil down to three truths what he had gleaned from his study of civilization.

First, he said there is a direct parallel between successful civilizations and the capacity of the societies to produce the capital investment that makes a productive society.

Second, a productive society creates institutions that are a source of both renewal and stability. They are the shelters of continuity.

Third, while nineteen of the past twenty-one civilizations collapsed from internal decay, there is no reason to assume collapse is an inevitable consequence if the people as individuals have the will.

And if I might boil all that down to one message, it is: Nourish spiritually and materially those institutions like this college which are the sustainers of civilization and shelters of continuity.

415   As Mark Twain said, "When some men discharge an obligation, you can hear the report for miles around." But, in the case of the people you see here, they did a job with no fanfare. . . .

416   In Webster's Unabridged Dictionary there is a clue to our troubled society. It devotes one hundred one column inches to the definition of "take" and thirty-five inches to "give." Fortunately for our society, there are those who do give more than take.

- Give financial help
- • Give their time
- • • Give their hearts

GENERAL

417   Almost everybody thought that Marshal Joffre had won the first battle of the Marne during World War I, but some refused to agree. One day a newspaperman appealed to Joffre: "Will you tell me who did win the battle of the Marne?" "I can't answer that," said the Marshal. "But I can tell you that if the battle of the Marne had been lost the blame would have been on me."

418   The government was contemplating the dispatch of an expedition to Burma, with a view to taking Rangoon, and a question arose as to who would be the fittest general to be sent in command of the expedition. The Cabinet sent for the Duke of Wellington, and asked his advice. He instantly replied, "Send Lord Combermere." "But we have always understood that Your Grace thought Lord Combermere a fool." "So he is a fool, and a damned fool; but he can take Rangoon."

419   General Omar Bradley once remarked that "the world has achieved brilliance without conscience."

420   I think it was King James who first said, "I can commission an officer, but only God can make a gentleman."

421   Count Leo Tolstoy once said that every general he ever met was either stupid or absent-minded. Well, I must be a little of both to . . .

422   General Dwight Eisenhower, who helped win World War II and who negotiated an end to the Korean War, once said this about the need for a strong defense: "In the final choice a soldier's pack is not so heavy a burden as a prisoner's chains."

423   Too much of military science is that remarkable act in which lessons learned in winning one war can, if strictly followed, lose the next.

424   In 1962 General Douglas MacArthur made his last trip to West Point. At the close of his address to the young cadets, he said, "In the evening of my memory, always I come back to West Point. Always there echoes and re-echoes in my ears— Duty—Honor—Country—When I cross the river my last conscious thoughts will be of the Corps—and the Corps—and the Corps."

425   In the Presbyterian Meeting House churchyard, Alexandria, Virginia, there is this tribute inscribed on the tomb of an unknown soldier of the Revolutionary War.

Here lies a soldier of
The Revolution whose identity
Is known but to God.
    His was an idealism
That recognized a Supreme
Being, that planted
Religious liberty on our
Shores, that overthrew
Despotism, that established
A people's government,
That wrote a Constitution
Setting metes and bounds
Of delegated authority,
That fixed a standard of
Value upon men above

Gold and lifted high the
Torch of civil liberty
Along the pathway of
Mankind.
　In ourselves his soul
Exists as part of ours,
His memory's mansion.

426　Over 160 years ago, Andrew Jackson, as a militia general, issued a proclamation to rouse the citizens of Tennessee against the threat from abroad which was to become the War of 1812. "Volunteer to Arms" he called that proclamation. He reminded the men of Tennessee that they were different from the "tilled slaves of George II, or the frozen peasants of Russia." "We are freeborn citizens," he said. "We are going to fight for the re-establishment of our national character."

427　In 325 B.C. Alexander the Great's march to India was halted by the flogging spirits of his troops, who wanted to turn back and go home to Macedonia. On the banks of Bibasa in India, Alexander told his men, overwhelmed by the hardships of a sustained march in a strange country: "When hardships are only steps to a goal, the courageous man calls them challenges."

428　The following was taken from General Orders of August 13, 1776, by George Washington: "The general therefore again repeats his earnest request, that every officer, and soldier, will have his arms and ammunition in good order, keep within his quarters and encampment, as much as possible; be ready for action at a moment's call; and when called to it, remember that liberty, property, life and honor are all at stake; upon their courage and conduct rest the hopes of their bleeding and insulted country; that their wives, children, and parents expect safety from them only, and that we have every reason to expect heaven will crown with success so just a cause."

429　During the Korean War, a young American prisoner was called out of the ranks by the Chinese captain, who said to him, "What do you think of General George C. Marshall?" He

said, "I think George Marshall is a great American." He was hit
by the butt of a rifle and knocked to the ground. They picked
him up and said, "What do you think of George Marshall now?"
He said, "I think George Marshall is a great American."

This time, there was no rifle butt because they had classified
him and determined upon his courage.

I think, as individuals and as Americans, we too are going to
be called to give an affirmative answer.

GENTLEMAN

430   In John O'Hara's novel *The Rage to Live* the character
called Sydney Tate says to his wife, "You see, in this world you
learn a set of rules, or you don't learn them. But assuming you
learn them, you stick by them."

GOVERNMENT OFFICIAL

431   I remember reading in Plutarch's *Lives* of a little old
lady who was refused a hearing by Alexander the Great. She
reprimanded him saying, "If you have no time for the little
person as well as the big, you have no time to be King." And,
similarly, the government official who has no time to consider
each citizen's request is not worthy of his position. Today I
would like to outline the various ways we have made our office
more accessible.

432   The French Minister Talleyrand once said the art of
administration is to foresee the inevitable and expedite its occurrence. Or in other words how are we adapting to future
trends?

    • Trends
    •• Measures and programs to meet those trends

433   Alexander Hamilton once wrote, "Energy in the executive is the leading character in the definition of good govern-

ment." In that case our speaker must single-handedly do much to raise the productivity of government. I know of few who are more active.

434   Someone described an administrator's role mostly as one of coordination. In that respect I like Vice-President Henry Wallace's definition of "coordinator" when Nelson Rockefeller was coordinator of Latin American Affairs. "A coordinator is a man who can keep all the balls in the air without losing his own." Certainly our speaker is one who keeps a lot of balls in the air—he is in charge of the following programs. . . .

435   As Dwight Eisenhower once remarked, "Only two types of problems come to my desk—one marked 'IMPORTANT' and the other marked 'URGENT' and I never get to the 'IMPORTANT'." So in the interests of time I would like to address myself to one of our more urgent problems.

436   In Robert Bolt's play *A Man for All Seasons,* Sir Thomas More says, "If ministers sacrifice their private conscience to popular opinion, they lead their country by a short route to chaos."

437   Justice Louis Brandeis once wrote, "The great America for which we long is unattainable unless the individuality of community is far more highly developed. The growth of the future must be in quality and spiritual value and that comes through the concentrated striving of small groups. If ideals are developed locally, the national ones will come pretty near taking care of themselves."

438   The Roman historian Tacitus thought the way to stay in office was to play safe and not to offer bold new plans. Well, despite Tacitus, I would like to offer a new program—one that may prompt a few questions but one that I think will offer the answer to some long-festering problems.

439   In the Old Testament, we remember how King Solomon, as a youth, was visited by an angel of the Lord. The angel asked the newly anointed King what he needed most to rule?"

Solomon replied, "Give me an understanding heart." As a public official our speaker has demonstrated a compassionate and understanding heart in the following ways . . .

440   Sir Anthony Eden once said, "Everyone is always in favor of general economy and particular expenditure."

441   It was a New Dealer and founder of his own government bureau who said, "The nearest thing to immortality in this world is a government bureau."

442   The mistake of too many bureaucrats is in forgetting they have been appointed and thinking they have been anointed.

443   It was Mark Twain who noted that in his home town he could always tell when there was going to be a speech by a public official because sales of eggs and vegetables picked up appreciably.

444   Ralph Waldo Emerson once had this warning for bureaucrats—treat people well, as if they are real; perhaps they are.

GRATEFUL PERSON

445   In *Richard II,* Shakespeare writes, "Evermore thanks, the exchequer of the poor." In other words, the most a poor man can do is say thank you.

446   In a letter to the Abbé Sicard, the French writer J. B. Massieu once wrote, "Gratitude is the memory of the heart."

GROOM

447   I feel I can say of my bride what Lord Randolph Churchill said of Jenny just before the parents of Winston Churchill married, "She is as nice, as lovable and amiable and charming in every way as she is beautiful and by her education

and bringing up she is in every way qualified to fill any position."

448   I know what Dr. Samuel Johnson said about marriage —"It may have some pains but celibacy has no pleasures whatsoever"—so it's the pleasures I'd like to address myself to . . .

GUEST

449   Our hostess makes you feel so much at home. She's like Perle Mesta, who used to greet guests saying, "At last" and when they left she said, "So soon." With similar grace . . .

450   The word "sayonara" in Japanese means more than "goodbye"—literally it means "if." The implied sentence is "If we have to—then let us part." And since the time has come for us to go, I would like to thank . . .

451   There is a Polish proverb that a guest sees more in an hour than a host in a year. So that gives me permission to comment on some things I have seen at this house this evening.

452   Almost twenty-five hundred years ago the Greek playwright Aeschylus wrote, "There is nothing warmer than the feeling between guest and host."

453   Prince Philip, the Duke of Edinburgh, said that the first responsibility of a good guest is to know when to leave.

454   It was the Roman historian Pliny who first wrote that home is where the heart is. In that case . . .

455   I recall a passage by Sinclair Lewis in *Babbitt:* "In fact there was but one thing wrong with the Babbitt house: It was not a home." But here we can say there is a home—a spirit of family and love.

456   It was said of Thomas Jefferson's White House that his hospitality combined Republican simplicity with epicurean delicacy.

457   An Irish blessing reads: "May the road rise to meet you. May the wind always be at your back. May the sun shine warm upon your face, the rains fall soft upon your fields. And until we meet again . . . may God hold you in the palm of his hand."

HEALTH WORKER

458   Thomas Jefferson said, "Health is the first requirement after morality."

459   As Mahatma Gandhi wrote, "It is health which is real wealth and not pieces of gold and silver."

460   Ben Jonson wrote: "O health! health! The blessing of the rich! The riches of the poor! Who can buy thee at too dear a rate, since there is no enjoying this world without thee?"

461   Florence Nightingale, the great nurse, was the first to advocate open windows in hospitals—letting in fresh air to the rooms full of germs and impurities.

HISTORIAN

462   The German scholar Schlegel wrote, "A historian is a prophet in reverse." So what insights and truths can we see in the last two hundred years.

463   In John Le Carré's *The Spy Who Came in from the Cold,* the protagonist Alec Leamas asks his girl what she believes in. She replies, "History." Today I would like to begin by tracing the history of this . . .

464   The philosopher Will Durant said, "If a man is fortunate he will, before he dies, gather up as much as he can of his civilized heritage and transmit it to his children." Tonight let us review some of that heritage.

465   Cicero once said, "He who is ignorant of what happened before his birth is always a child."

466   The great Spanish philosopher Ortega y Gasset puts it this way, "Any explanation of the visible changes appearing on the surface of history which does not go deep down until it touches the mysterious and latent changes produced in the depths of the human soul is superficial." Each person, therefore, must first work on himself before his improved understanding can radiate to those in his orbit.

467   Aldous Huxley once wrote, "Life has to be lived forwards; but it can only be understood backwards. I suppose that's why we always make the important discoveries too late."

468   It was H. L. Mencken who said a historian was just an unsuccessful novelist.

469   During an address in Pittsburgh, Dwight D. Eisenhower said, "The history of free men is never really written by chance but by choice—their choice."

470   In a speech in Richmond, Virginia, Adlai Stevenson remarked, "We can chart our future clearly and wisely only when we know the path which has led to the present."

471   The French philosopher Raymond Aron has written, "Historical understanding consists of perceiving differences among similar phenomena and similarities among different phenomena."

472   In *Mrs. Miniver,* Jan Struther wrote: "In the convex driving-mirror [Mrs. Miniver] could see, dwindling rapidly, the patch of road where they had stood; and she wondered why it had never occurred to her before that you cannot successfully navigate the future unless you keep always framed beside it a small clear image of the past."

HOST

473   At a great dinner, Samuel Johnson once said, "It isn't so much what's on the table that matters as what's on the chairs." And tonight we have some distinguished guests.

474   Horace once wrote that a host is like a general; calamities often reveal whether he has genius. Well, tonight certain disasters have exposed my true colors.

475   It was said of the man of letters Frank Harris that he was invited to all the great houses in England—once. Happily, that is not the case . . .

HUSBAND

476   James Thurber once said, "Love is what you've been through with somebody."

477   Shortly after General Washington assumed the Continental Army command in Cambridge, Massachusetts, his wife joined him from Mount Vernon. At a dinner celebrating her return, General Washington raised his glass, "To you, my dearest, for giving me the strength I need to have to carry on."

478   I used to vow never to marry until I found the ideal woman. Well, when I found her, alas, I found out she was looking for the perfect man.

479   I think Notre Dame's Father Hesburgh had good advice: "The most important thing a father can do for his children is to love their mother."

480   I told my brother years ago that I would give him all the advice he wanted provided he would agree not to take it. Shortly after I was married I volunteered some worthy advice and counsel to my wife, who listened with tolerance and then inquired if I had ever heard of Oscar Wilde's observation: "All advice is bad and good advice is worse."

JOURNALIST

481 When Ralph McGill, the late editor of the Atlanta *Constitution,* was asked how it felt to be awarded the recognition as America's foremost journalist, he said, "Frustrated—frustrated that so little has been changed by so many words."

482 Teddy Roosevelt once said, "A good journalist should be part St. Paul and part St. Vitus." A good editor today must be part Santa Claus, part St. Valentine, part St. Thomas (the doubter), part St. Paul, and certainly he must be part St. Jude. St. Jude, as you know, is the patron saint of those who ask for the impossible.

483 The Swiss philosopher Amiel observed, "Truth is violated by falsehood, but it is outraged by silence." Let us rescue truth from outrage.

484 The problem for a journalist is like the question asked by George Webber in Thomas Wolfe's *You Can't Go Home Again:* "What is truth? No wonder jesting Pilate turned away. The truth, it has a thousand faces—show only one of them, and the whole truth flies away! But how to show the whole? That's the question."

485 As Brendan Gill wrote of his *New Yorker* editor Harold Ross, "Ross clung to the facts as a shipwrecked man clings to a spar." Another similar fact clinger is the man we honor tonight.

486 On John O'Hara's gravestone there is engraved this epitaph: "Better than anyone else, he told the truth about his time. . . . He was a professional. He wrote honestly and well." Our next speaker also lives up to those words.

487 When the French writer Albert Camus received the Nobel Prize for literature, he was asked what makes a job a vocation. He replied, "The two trusts that constitute the nobility of one's service—the service of truth and the service of

freedom." Our next speaker has served the cause of freedom by serving the cause of truth.

488   Back in the eighteenth century, Jonathan Swift warned of journalists and reporters who mistake the echo of a London coffeehouse for the voice of the people. This is not true of our next speaker, who is an investigative reporter.

489   I thank the chairman for his gracious introduction. I might add that most people don't feel as kindly toward the newspaper profession. Many people feel like Oscar Wilde, who said, "In old days they had the rack. Now they have the press."

490   Winston Churchill once leveled two criticisms at America. He said, "The problem with America is that their toilet paper is too thin and their newspapers too fat." Seriously, I am glad when the newspaper gives me extensive coverage on an assignment—just as I am glad that you offered me the opportunity to speak today.

491   Sydney Smith about 150 years ago said there are three things that every man thinks he can do—namely, drive a gig, farm a property, and edit a newspaper.

492   It was a journalist, William Lloyd Garrison, who said, "I am in earnest—I shall not equivocate—I shall not excuse—I shall not retreat a single word—and I shall be heard."

493   It was Finley Peter Dunne's Irish bartender Mr. Dooley who observed that the job of the reporter was to comfort the afflicted and afflict the comfortable.

494   Clement Attlee of Britain once said, "The press lives on disaster."

495   "A reporter," said Edward R. Murrow, "is always concerned with tomorrow. There's nothing tangible of yesterday."

496   James Reston of the *New York Times* once explained news this way: "If it's far away, it's news, but if it's close at home, it's sociology."

497   Christopher Morley got to the heart of the life of a newspaperman when he said that truth for the day-to-day journalist is not a solid but a fluid.

498   In 1787 Thomas Jefferson wrote to a friend that the people must be given full information on their nation's affairs "through the channels of the public papers," and that "these papers should penetrate the whole mass of the people." He added: "Were it left to me to decide whether we should have a government without newspapers, or newspapers without a government, I should not hesitate a moment to prefer the latter. But I should mean that every man should receive these papers and be capable of reading them."

JUDGE

499   Justice Felix Frankfurter was once asked if a man changes when he goes on the bench. He replied, "If he is any good, he does." Well, I know my views have changed. For one thing they have changed on the subject of the likelihood of rehabilitation.

500   One of the great judicial insights was provided by Oliver Wendell Holmes. He was asked by a reporter the secret of his successful judicial career. "Young man," said Holmes, "the secret of my success is that at a very early age I discovered I am not God."

501   Justice Louis Brandeis once said, "Nine-tenths of the serious controversies which arise in life result from misunderstanding. They result from one man not knowing the facts which to the other man seem important or otherwise failing to appreciate his point of view." Today I would like to examine a set of facts which concern those who have the responsibility of prosecuting our criminals.

502   Former Supreme Court Justice Robert Jackson once wrote: "You must remember that not every defeat of author-

ity is a gain for individual freedom nor every judicial rescue of a convict a victory for liberty." Jackson recognized the court's difficult task of finding a middle course between the extremes of anarchy and totalitarianism or the problem of defending the rights of the accused without endangering society.

503   Oliver Wendell Holmes once described his role as judge, "It's quiet here but the quiet of a storm center." Today I would like to discuss one storm center in society.

504   The Greeks had a saying about justice. Justice not only must be done but must be seen to be done. Today the revolving-door process with criminal defendants, the rapes and muggings by those out on bail, the light sentences, etc. are seen by citizens as a failure of justice.

505   The late Justice Felix Frankfurter came back from Russia shocked by the speed of their system. The judges there would try a man in five minutes. "You are a reactionary? To Siberia! You are half a reactionary? To prison!" So, while we condemn the delays of court process, we must recognize that some of these delays are the price of protection of democratic liberties.

506   Andrew Jackson made a good judge in Tennessee, and though his knowledge of legal technicalities was a bit sketchy his charge to juries has become a classic: "Do what is right between these parties. That is what the law always means." And that is what it should always mean.

507   Sam Ervin, a former judge as well as a Senator, once said: "As lawyers we know this. The law requires all laymen to know every bit of the law; it requires lawyers to know a reasonable amount of the law, but it does not require judges to know a doggone thing."

508   The Zapatic Indians of Mexico have a very sophisticated concept of justice. In their tribal system the function of

the judge is to maneuver the parties into a compromise which they both will accept.

509   The quality of justice in the frontier West was so bad that the word for "court" became synonymous with "jail." "Hoosegow," the Western slang for "jail," came from the Spanish *juzgado*, the word for a court or tribunal. Today rights of criminals have come almost to mean the release of criminal suspects.

510   The English Justice, Lord Chatty, once described the cost of civil suits. He said, "Certainly the courts are open to all —just like the Ritz Hotel." Today I would like to talk about the expense of civil trials, particularly jury trials.

511   Finley Peter Dunne has his Irish bartender Mr. Dooley say, "Justice is blind. Blind she is, an' deef an' dumb an' has a wooden leg."

512   Thomas Clark once said that justice is everybody's business—it affects every man's fireside; it passes on his property, his reputation, his liberty, his life.

513   Earl Warren's trademark on the bench was to intercept the lawyer's legal argument with a simple, almost naïve question. "Yes, but is it fair?" He believed that social justice is more important than legalisms.

514   When Judge Learned Hand once said to Oliver Wendell Holmes that "we have a court of justice," Justice Holmes said "No, we have a court of law." And he explained that laws are the tools to achieve the ideal of justice.

515   In *A Man for All Seasons*, the character Will Roper said he would cut down every law in England to get the Devil. Thomas More replied, "Oh? And when the last law was down, and the Devil turned round on you—where would you hide, Roper, the laws all being flat? This country's planted thick with laws from coast to coast and if you cut them down—and you're just the man to do it—d'you really think you could stand upright

in the winds that would blow then?" Similarly the laws protecting the criminally accused protect us—protect us as individuals who are innocent from unfair harassment by the state.

516   New Jersey Justice Alfred T. Vanderbilt once said, "We need judges learned in the law, not merely the law in books but something far more difficult to acquire, the law as applied in action; judges deeply versed in the system of human nature and adept in the discovery of the truth in the discordant testimony of fallible human beings."

517   Chief Justice Charles Evans Hughes once wrote: "The most ominous sign of our time is the indication of the growth of an intolerant spirit. It is the more dangerous when armed, as it usually is, with sincere conviction. . . . Our institutions were not devised to bring about uniformity of opinion; if they had been, we might well abandon hope. It is important to remember that the essential characteristic of true liberty is that under its shelter, many different types of life and character and opinion and belief can develop unmolested and unobstructed."

518   The guards at the jail in Alamos, Mexico, may well be the most vigilant in the world. They have regulations at Alamos which provide that a guard must serve out the sentence of any prisoner who escapes while he is on duty. The practice might be applied to judges who give suspended sentences to rapists or muggers who then might repeat their crimes.

519   Finley Peter Dunne has his Irish bartender, Mr. Dooley, say, "If I had me a job to pick out, I'd be a judge. I've looked over all th' others an' that's the only one that suits. I have th' judicyal temperament. I hate wurruk."

520   Justice Benjamin Cardozo wrote, "The great tides and currents which engulf the rest of men, do not turn aside in their course and pass the judges by."

521   The best description of justice was given by a Judge Dalton, who said a judge must be courageous enough to give the devil his due whether he is in the right or in the wrong.

522   Alexander Hamilton wrote in his *Federalist Papers* that the judiciary was the weakest of the three branches of government because it had neither the sword of the executive nor the purse of the legislature—it had neither force nor will, only judgment.

523   Justice Cardozo said, "The judge must be an historian and prophet all in one."

524   Chief Justice Earl Warren wrote, "Our judges are not monks or scientists but participants in the living stream of our national life."

525   "Justice," wrote Disraeli, "is truth in action."

526   The French philosopher Blaise Pascal wrote, "Justice without power is inefficiency; power without justice is tyranny."

527   William Penn wrote, "Justice is the insurance we have on our lives and property; obedience is the premium we pay for it."

528   In 1798 James Madison proposed a toast to the Federal judiciary, "May it remember that it is the Expositor of the laws, and not the Trumpeter of politics."

529   A wise commentator once said, "The judge who does not agonize before passing sentence is a criminal."

530   Justice Benjamin Cardozo wrote, "The heroic hours of life do not announce their presence by drum and trumpet, challenging us to be true to ourselves by appeals to the martial spirit that keeps the blood at heat. Some little, unassuming, unobtrusive choice presents itself before us slyly and craftily, glib and insinuating, in the modest garb of innocence. To yield to its blandishments is so easy. The wrong, it seems, is venial. . . . Then it is that you will be summoned to show the courage of adventurous youth."

531   Justice Oliver Wendell Holmes wrote, "Historic continuity with the past is not a duty, it is only a necessity."

532   Justice Alfred Vanderbilt noted that "judicial reform is no sport for the short-winded."

LABOR LEADER

533   One of the first walkouts was one of bricklayers—Moses and Aaron led them out against their Egyptian employers. Injustice then and injustice now is what a strike is all about.

534   In Greece where democracy began, there were unions or guilds called "Thiasoses"—of stonemasons, potters, actors, dockers, etc.

535   A century ago, Samuel Gompers was asked what were the goals of the American labor movement. He answered in one word, "More." Asked what he meant by "more," he answered, More wages, more holidays, more benefits." Today it is not so much quantity but quality—what kind of conditions, what kind of job security.

536   When Eugene Debs was jailed in Chicago during the Pullman strike, he received this telegram: "Stand by your principles regardless of consequences. Your Father and Mother." Today I would like to talk about the labor principles that Debs as well as the rest of us chose to live by.

- Healthy conditions
- • Decent wages
- • • Free bargaining

LAWYER

537   The Roman lawyer Cicero explained the rule of law this way: "We are in bondage to the law in order that we may be free."

- No one above the law
- • Change laws by democratic process
- • • Without law, anarchy

538   Abraham Lincoln once wrote, "It is as the peacemaker that the lawyer has the superior opportunity to be a great man."

539   According to Dean Roscoe Pound there are six rules that make a vocation a profession:

(1) The mastery of special skills and methods
(2) Knowledge of scholarly, historical, or scientific principles
(3) Long and intensive preparation and a commitment to continuing study
(4) High standards of achievement and conduct
(5) A personal freedom and independence of ideas
(6) A sense of dedication to public service.

540   In *The Ox-Bow Incident,* Walter Van Tilburg Clark wrote: "Law is more than the words that put it on the books; law is more than any decisions that may be made from it; law is more than the particular code of it stated at any one time or in any one place or nation; more than any man, lawyer or judge, sheriff or jailer, who may represent it. True law, the code of justice, the essence of our sensations of right and wrong, is the conscience of society. It has taken thousands of years to develop, and it is the greatest, the most distinguishing quality which has evolved with mankind. None of man's temples, none of his religions, none of his weapons, his tools, his arts, his sciences, nothing else he has grown to, is so great a thing as his justice, his sense of justice. The true law is something in itself; it is the spirit of the moral nature of man; it is an existence apart, like God, and as worthy of worship as God. If we can touch God at all, where do we touch him save in the conscience? And what is the conscience of any man save his little fragment of the conscience of all men in all time?"

541   New Jersey Supreme Court Chief Justice Alfred Vanderbilt said: "The great lawyer has four functions: First, he is a wise counsellor to all manner of men. Second, he is an advocate skilled in procedure, techniques and forensic arts. Third, as a member of a worthy calling, he has an obligation to upbuild that

profession. Fourth, every great lawyer in a free society has a responsibility to act as an intelligent, unselfish leader of public opinion within his particular sphere of interest." In all of these roles our speaker eminently . . .

542   When Abraham Lincoln made his way from Springfield to Washington to be inaugurated as the sixteenth President, he often made speeches from the back of the train to citizens at various cities. At one stop, he told them that the future of democracy depended on the commitment of each of them. "I appeal to you to constantly bear in mind that not with the politicians, not with the President, not with the office-seekers, but with you is the question, 'Shall the liberties of this country be preserved to the latest generations.' "

543   It was the lawyer and statesman Edmund Burke who differentiated between what is legal and what is right. "It is not what a lawyer tells me I may do, but what humanity, reason, and justice tell me I ought to do."

544   It is said that ministers deal with moral law or those spiritually sick, and doctors deal with the natural law and those physically sick, and we lawyers deal with the civil law or those socially sick.

545   Sir Walter Scott said a lawyer without some knowledge of history or literature is a mechanic, a mere working mason; if he possesses some knowledge of these, he may venture to call himself an architect.

546   Balboa, the Spanish explorer, wrote to King Ferdinand asking him to prohibit the entry of lawyers into the new world.

547   Justice Holmes said that all able lawyers fall into three categories: butcher knives, razors, and stings.

548   The historian Edward Gibbon wrote about a man who well remembered he had a retainer to collect and only forgot he had a duty to perform.

549   Shakespeare knew that you can't set up a totalitarian state unless you get rid of all the lawyers. In *Henry VI* he has

the plotter, Dick the Butcher, say, "The first thing we do, let's kill all the lawyers."

550   In *Pickwick Papers,* the attorney says of a colleague, "Yes, he is a very young man. He was only called the other day. Let me see—oh, he hasn't been at the bar eight years yet."

551   As Rufus Choate said, "The lawyer's vacation is the space between the question put to a witness and his answer."

552   Justice Oliver Wendell Holmes once wrote, "If you want to hit a bird on the wing, you must have all your will in a focus. You must not be thinking about yourself, and equally you must not be thinking about your neighbor; you must be living with your eye on that bird. Every achievement is a bird on the wing."

553   Sir Arthur Bryant, the British historian, wrote: "In reality, the man who defies or flouts the law is like the proverbial fool who saws away the plank on which he sits, and a disrespect or disregard for law is always the first sign of a disintegrating society. Respect for law is the most fundamental of all social virtues, for the alternative to the rule of law is that of violence and anarchy."

554   Reminiscing once about his long and distinguished career in the law, Felix Frankfurter pointedly recalled how a dispute over a legal question had ended with a colleague on the Harvard Law School faculty. "You take law awfully seriously," his friend chided him. "Yes," Professor Frankfurter replied quietly, "that's one accusation against which I plead guilty without reservation. I do take law very seriously," he maintained, "because fragile as reason is and limited as law is as the expression of the institutionalized medium of reason, that's all we have standing between us and tyranny of mere will and the cruelty of unbridled, undisciplined feeling."

555   At Thingvellir in Iceland stands the Law Rock, where in 930 the Althing, the Parliament, was formed. The Law

Speaker there was required to read aloud the entire legal code, one third each year.

556   In *The Taming of the Shrew,* Shakespeare wrote, "Do as adversaries do in law—Strive mightily, but eat and drink as friends."

557   In *A Man for All Seasons,* Robert Bolt writes, "The law is a causeway upon which, so long as he keeps to it, a citizen may walk safely."

558   In *Measure for Measure,* Shakespeare wrote:

> We must not make a scarecrow of the law,
> Setting it up to fear the birds of prey,
> And let it keep one shape, till custom make it
> Their perch, and not their terror.

559   In his "blood, sweat, and tears" speech Winston Churchill said: "Civilization means a society based upon the opinion of civilians. It means that violence, the rule of warriors and despotic chiefs, the conditions of camps and warfare, of riot and tyranny, give place to parliaments where laws are made, and independent courts of justice in which over long periods those laws are maintained."

560   The origin of the phrase "Philadelphia lawyer" is for many people unknown, yet the man who inspired the term was one who was called "the Morning Star of the Revolution." Colonial lawyer Andrew Hamilton of Philadelphia saw early dangers in the developing tyranny of the British government. In his courageous and eloquent defense of printer John Peter Zenger in New York City in 1735, he described the perils of remote, impersonal, insensitive government. "Power may justly be compared to a great river; while kept within its bounds it is both powerful and useful, but when it overflows its banks it is then too impetuous to be stamped. It bears down on the ford and brings destruction and desolation wherever it comes. If then this be the nature of power let us at least do our duty like wise men using our utmost care to support liberty."

LEGISLATOR

561   Senator Everett Dirksen once said, "Congress is like a waterlogged scow. It doesn't go too far. It doesn't go fast. But it doesn't sink." That saying reflects this year's record of Congress—we didn't get around to acting on some problems we should have. On the other hand, we defeated a lot of hasty, ill-considered bills not really in the public interest.

562   Theodore Roosevelt used to say, "Representative government is that which elects six men in favor of a thing and six against it and wonders why something isn't done." That is not a good excuse for this year's legislative record by Congress, but it does help to explain that bills, where strong interests conflict, are not easily passed. Let's take for example some bills which I was interested in.

563   Henry Adams once had a character in a novel say, "If I ever turn anarchist, it will be for the fun of murdering a senator." Even if for obvious reasons, I think that is rather drastic action. I can sympathize with the frustrations of some people, particularly when I consider the Senate's disappointing record this year.

564   The ancient Greek statesman Solon was once asked, "Did you write the best laws for Athens?" "No," said Solon. "Only the best that could be enacted." And that explains my attitude toward the recent legislation which I sponsored.

565   In 1787 George Washington implored the Constitutional delegates at Philadelphia, "Let us raise a standard to which the wise and honest can repair." What Washington, who presided over the Constitutional Convention was saying at that time was, Let's find a way that will eliminate the evils and excesses without inhibiting or punishing the decent and good. That is precisely my aim in opposing some of the provisions in this current bill under debate.

566   The great first-act closer in *Of Thee I Sing* featured the bouncy number "Love Is Sweeping the Country." And then the leading character, John Wintergreen, adds in a stage whisper, "Believe me, this country could stand a good sweeping." Similarly, today I would like to talk about three bills of reform legislation which I have sponsored.

567   In ancient Rome the writer Polybius told Senators their best training was to study history. In other words history was better than theory. Tonight I would like to outline the records . . .

568   Patrick Henry, in the Virginia House of Burgesses, said, "I know of no way of judging the future save by the past." Let us see what has happened to those who followed . . .

569   I find that old Gilbert and Sullivan ditty a little too true in its description of the legislative process,

> The House of Peers through out the war
> Did nothing in particular
> And did it very well.

570   Not all the Capitol chaplains were perfunctory. The Reverend Byron Sunderland, one day in April, 1864, invoked: "O Lord, give us that Thou wilt in Thine infinite wisdom vouchsafe to our rulers and legislators in this Congress assembled more brains—more brains, Lord."

571   Mark Twain once commented, "It could probably be shown by facts and figures that there is no distinctly native American criminal class except Congress."

572   In his *Reflections on the Revolution in France,* Edmund Burke wrote, "A state without some means of change is without the means of its conservation."

573   James I would say to the lords of his council, when they sat upon any great matter, and came to him from council, "Well, you have sat, but what have you hatched?"

574   Edmund Burke once commented, "There are two, and only two, foundations of law . . . equity and utility."

LOSER

575   In Alabama they say defeated politicians head for Buck's Pocket—that's an Alabama expression meaning a place where politicians go to nurse their wounds and wait for the next time.

576   In this Bicentennial period I like to recall the words of General Nathanael Greene to the French Ambassador in 1781 to explain the eventual American success: "We fight, get beat, rise—fight again." So we may have lost a battle but we haven't lost a war.

577   I am not ashamed of defeat. Like the doctor in Albert Camus's story when asked if he would like to retire to a cloister to become a saint: "No," the doctor said, "I feel more fellowship with the defeated than the saints. Heroism and sanctity don't really appeal to me—what interests me is being a man." So I am going to wear the stripes of defeat proudly—they are the stripes of strife, struggle, and service.

578   As Abraham Lincoln said when he was once defeated, "I feel like the boy in Kentucky who stubbed his toe while he was running to see his sweetheart. The boy said he was too big to cry and far too badly hurt to laugh."

579   Of course I am unhappy about the defeat. But I have great faith in the country and its future. As John Quincy Adams wrote in his diary after his defeat by Andrew Jackson, "The sun of my political life may have set, but that of my country shines unclouded." And similarly, I have not lost faith in the future.

580   There is an old German proverb which says,

> Wealth lost, something lost;
> Honor lost, much lost;
> Courage lost, all lost.

Well, I may have lost some wealth, but I still hold my head high, not afraid to fight again.

581   After his defeat in the 1952 presidential campaign, Adlai Stevenson commented in an address to a group of reporters, "I have great faith in the people. As to their wisdom, well, Coca-Cola still outsells champagne."

582   My reaction to the election is much like the story John Kennedy told when he was defeated for the vice-presidential nomination in 1956. He said, "I feel like the Indian who had a lot of arrows stuck in him, and when he was asked how it felt, said, 'It only hurts when I laugh.' "

583   Thomas Edison sank a fortune into his great film studio. The building caught fire and burned to the ground, all his years of work gone up in flames. Edison broke silence: "Gentlemen, we start building tomorrow."

584   I am reminded of the line in Jason Miller's play *That Championship Season.* The old coach tells his former player, "Pain is the price of success. You got to have pain to succeed."

585   As the Polish patriot Josef Pilsudski said, "To be vanquished and not surrender—that is victory."

586   The French philosopher Blaise Pascal once wrote, "We act as though it were our mission to bring about the triumph of truth, but our mission is only to fight for it."

587   I would like to close with the words of Theodore Roosevelt: "It is not the critic who counts, not the one who points out how the strong man stumbled or how the doer of deeds might have done them better. The credit belongs to the man who is actually in the arena, whose face is marred with sweat and dust and blood; who strives valiantly, who errs and comes short again and again; who knows the great enthusiasms, the great devotions, and spends himself in a worthy cause; who, if he wins, knows the triumph of high achievement, and who, if he fails, at

least fails while daring greatly, so that his place shall never be with those cold and timid souls who know neither victory nor defeat."

588 We may have been defeated but as actor Anthony Quinn said about a play that closed early, "I'd rather play in a bomb by Tennessee Williams than be in a hit by a shit."

589 In John Patrick's play *The Teahouse of the August Moon,* the interpreter Sakini speaks with Captain Fisby, saying, "They say—explain what is Democracy. . . ." Fisby replied, "Well, it's a system of self-determination. It's—It's the right to make the wrong choice."

LOVER

590 Robert Burns wrote,

> To see her is to love her,
> And love but her forever;
> For nature made her what she is,
> And ne'er made sic anither!

591 I know of no better definition of love than the one given by Proust: "Love is space and time measured by the heart."

592 The mystery writer John MacDonald once gave this test for love—when a physical flaw or imperfection looks very dear to you, you know you are in very deep.

593 As one test for love, Somerset Maugham had a mother say to her daughter in the play *The Constant Wife,* "My dear, I only know one test. Could you use his toothbrush?" Well, we haven't shared a toothbrush, but we have shared . . .

594 If I were a singer, I would sing Rosina's aria in Rossini's *Barber of Seville*—"une voce poco fa—there's a voice within my heart." And the voice tells me . . .

595   The last words of Goethe's *Faust* are, "Das Ewig-Weib-liche zieht us hinan—the precious essence of woman lifts us upward."

MANAGEMENT EXPERT

596   Charles Kettering, the famous General Motors engineer, once said, "A problem well stated is a problem half solved." So I would define our problem this way. . . .

597   The philosopher Alfred North Whitehead once put it this way: "Style is the ultimate morality of the mind. The administrator with a sense of style hates waste; the engineer with a sense of style economizes his material; the artisan with a sense of style prefers good work." The problem today is to reorganize the company to suit modern needs and eliminate old inefficiencies.

598   Joe Mankiewicz once told of the production problems of that colossal waste-film failure *Cleopatra*. "This picture was conceived in a state of emergency, shot in confusion and wound up in blind panic." Now, if we don't want to end up with similar foul-ups and failures, let us take a minute to stand back and assess where we are going and what is our real goal.

599   Alexander Hamilton wrote, "I mean to prepare the way for futurity."

600   I recall a cartoon strip in Charlie Schulz's *Peanuts* with Linus, holding his security blanket, saying, "No problem is so big or so complicated that it can't be run away from."

601   Scipio Africanus, the Roman general who conquered Carthage, once said, "In military affairs, 'I didn't think of it' is a disgrace."

602   In his *Lives of the Caesars*, Suetonius writes how the Emperor Titus confided to friends at a dinner: "Colleagues, I

have lost a day". He was reflecting how a day had passed without any constructive action being taken or any progress being made.

MARRIAGE

603   Dr. David Reuben once said, "A marriage is like a long trip in a tiny row boat: if one passenger starts to rock the boat, the other has to steady it; otherwise they will go to the bottom together."

604   I agree with Jean Kerr, who asked why Ralph Nader didn't investigate marriage. Nothing could be more unsafe than that.

605   As André Maurois said, "Marriage is an edifice that must be rebuilt every day."

MEDIA PERSONALITY

606   The poet W. H. Auden once said that all the mass media offers is not popular art but entertainment to be consumed like food, forgotten, and replaced by a new dish.

607   The critic John Mason Brown once wrote, "Some television programs are so much chewing gum for the eyes."

608   The British observer Alistair Cooke made this assessment of the impact of television. "Because of television we are getting more information than we can cope with. I think that's the reason for the sort of low-key hysteria—Thoreau's 'quiet desperation' that a lot of us live in."

MOTHER

609   Today I feel the way the Roman matriarch Cornelia did. Someone asked her where her jewels were. "Those are my

jewels," she said, pointing to her children. Well, my pride today has a glow brighter than any gems.

610   Peter De Vries once described the mother's lot: "A suburban mother's role," he said, "is to deliver children—obstetrically once and by car forever after." And it seems like I spent half my life chauffeuring to scout meetings, football games, skating lessons. But today it seems worth every minute of it.

PARENT

611   It is said parents are people who *bear* children, *bore* teenagers, and *board* newlyweds.

612   There is a French proverb that a father is a banker provided by God.

613   The New England writer Margaret Fuller once wrote, "The character, history and development of each child may be a poetic experience to the parent, if only he will allow it."

614   As Harry Truman once said, "I have found the best way to give advice to your children is to find out what they want and then advise them to do it."

615   George Bernard Shaw once wrote, "Parentage is a very important profession; but no test of fitness for it is ever imposed in the interest of the children."

616   Before I was married I had four theories about bringing up children; now I have four children and no theories.

617   The Duke of Windsor once said that the thing that most impressed him about America was the way parents obeyed their children.

618   I remember a friend of mine when growing up—he had every toy his father wanted.

PASTOR

619   The other day I saw a church message on the signboard outside a Manhattan church: COME IN—AND HAVE YOUR FAITH LIFTED.

• Lift your faith—member in a church
•• Lift your faith—prayer

620   Let us be mindful of the words of Saint Augustine, "I shall work as if everything depended on me. I shall pray as if everything depended on God."

621   George Fox, the seventeenth-century Quaker leader, once said, "Don't call the steeple-house the church. The church is the people." The church is not in the bricks and mortar but in the hearts and souls . . .

622   Today it seems the only time the clergy is needed is at marriages and funerals. I recall reading about the time the Anglican Bishop of Ripon was a dinner guest at Crathorne Hall in Yorkshire. Lady Crathorne said to the bishop, "How does it feel to belong to a dying industry?" But, seriously, spiritual needs have a relevance to modern life.

623   Pope John XXIII used this phrase to launch the Vatican II Congress: "I intend to open a window." He intended to open to discussion certain practices and doctrines of the church. Today I would like to air some doctrines we take for granted.

624   Faith is a difficult concept to define. Perhaps Reinhold Niebuhr's response to Justice Felix Frankfurter best describes it. After listening to his sermon Frankfurter said, "I liked what you said, Reinie, and I speak as a believing unbeliever." "I'm glad you did," Niebuhr replied, "for I spoke as an unbelieving believer." What Niebuhr meant is that faith transcends any Sunday-school concepts—one does not have to believe in all the trappings to grasp the basic presence of God.

625   The English novelist Samuel Butler once said a clergyman was expected to be a kind of human Sunday. That suggests we tune the church out on a Monday or a Saturday night—that in our neat and tidy worlds we can pay respects to the spiritual world by shaking hands with our minister on Sunday.

626   There is a French saying that there are three sexes—men, women, and clergymen. Which implies that priests are not of this world—not in tune or in touch with everyday bread-and-butter problems.

627   The last words of Pope John XXIII on May 31, 1963, were those of Christ after the Last Supper, "Ut unum sint—Let there be one." And let us today recognize that there is a oneness that transcends all our creeds and faiths.

628   Sir Kenneth Clark says in his lecture on "Civilization": "Heroic materialism is not enough." Art, he suggests, is a "reflection of a reflection" and an echo of God's presence and force in lifting the human soul.

629   On the wall of a New York subway station, a recent graffito read: "God is dead, s/g Nietzsche." To this, some subterranean pilgrim made the reply, "Nietzsche is dead. s/g God." People saying God is dead does not render him so. God lives in each one of us if we want to hear him—to respond—to act.

630   "Do you want to know what Hasidism is?" asks the Baal Shem-Tov, the eighteenth-century founder of the movement, in a story retold by Elie Wiesel in "Souls on Fire." And then in true Hasidic fashion he proceeds to tell a story himself. It is about an ironmonger who buys an anvil, a hammer, and a bellows and starts to go through the motions of his trade. But nothing happens. Perplexed, he asks the advice of an elderly colleague, who tells him, "You have everything you need except the spark." "That," concludes the Baal Shem-Tov, "is what Hasidism is: the spark."

631   Harvey Cox once said, "To celebrate the person today, religion will have to become more, not less, political. Churches

will have to expose governmental programs that increase people's dependency and deepen their sense of powerlessness."

632   In the 1930s a German pastor wrote: "When the Nazis came to arrest the Jews, I did not protest because I was not one of them. When they came to arrest the Communists, I did not protest because I was not one of them. When they arrested the Catholics, I did not protest because I was not one of them. When they arrested Socialist leaders, I did not protest, because I was not one of them. So, when they came to arrest Protestant ministers, there was no one left to stand up for me."

633   In one of her last entries in her diary Anne Frank wrote: "It's really a wonder that I haven't dropped all my ideals, because they seem so absurd and impossible to carry out. Yet I keep them, because in spite of everything, I still believe that people are really good at heart."

634   In Graham Greene's *The Heart of the Matter* Father Rank said, "For goodness' sake, Mrs. Scobie, don't imagine you —or I—know a thing about God's mercy." "The Church says . . ." "I know the Church says. The Church knows all the rules. But it doesn't know what goes on in a single human heart."

635   There is a line in *Of Human Bondage* which I am constantly reminded of. "There's always one who loves and one who lets himself be loved."

636   As Billy Graham once said, "I don't know what the future holds, but I know who holds the future."

637   The Spanish philosopher José Ortega y Gasset said about religion, "To believe in God is to yearn for His existence, and furthermore, it is to act as if He did exist."

638   The expert on statistics George Gallup once said, "I could prove God statistically. Take the human body alone—the chance that all the functions of the individual would just happen is a statistical monstrosity."

639   "The heart of religion," Martin Luther wrote, "lies in its personal pronouns."

640   T. S. Eliot once wrote, "Destiny waits in the hand of God, not in the hands of statesmen."

641   The Presbyterian minister Dr. Joseph Sizoo once said in a sermon, "The church that is married to the spirit of the age will find itself a widow in the next generation."

642   In the early church Augustine of Hippo wrote of his own bout with God: "I could give no reply except a lazy and drowsy 'Yes, Lord, yes. I'll get to it right away—just don't bother me for a little while.' But 'right away' didn't happen right away; and a 'little while' turned out to be a long while."

643   In Marc Connelly's *Green Pastures,* Noah says to God, "Lawd, I'm yo' servant. I ain't very much but I'se all I got."

644   At the close of World War I, the son of a Presbyterian minister, Woodrow Wilson, said, "The world cannot be saved materially unless it is redeemed spiritually."

645   It is said God will not look you over for medals, awards, degrees, or diplomas, but for scars.

646   The Post-Impressionist artist Vincent van Gogh once said that to believe in God is to feel that there is a God, not a dead one, or a stuffed one, but a living one, who with irresistible force urges us toward more loving.

647   In Owen Wister's *The Virginian* the cowboy says, "A middlin' doctor is a pore thing, and a middlin' lawyer is a pore thing, but keep me from a middlin' man of God."

648   The historian Will Durant writes: "The great question of our time is not Communism versus individualism; not East versus West—it is whether man can bear to live without God."

649   One of the early Christians, Augustine of Hippo, wrote, "God is an infinite circle whose center is everywhere and whose circumference is nowhere."

650   Too many ministers, to quote the old Gilbert and Sullivan ditty, are too "fond of uttering platitudes/In stained-glass attitudes."

651   Dr. Benjamin Jowett, the famous master of Balliol College, Oxford, was met one day by an undergraduate, who informed him that he could find no positive evidence of the existence of God. "Well," said Dr. Jowett, "if you do not find a God by five o'clock this afternoon, you will leave this college!"

652   In the play *The Great God Brown,* Eugene O'Neill wrote, "Man is born broken. He lives by mending. The grace of God is glue."

653   When Oliver Cromwell first coined his money, an old Cavalier, looking at one of the new pieces, read this inscription on one side, "God is with us." On the other, "The Commonwealth of England." "I see," said he, "that God and the Commonwealth are on different sides."

654   On April 2, 1945, Dietrich Bonhoeffer, the German Lutheran leader, said to a fellow prisoner that "it was his duty not only to comfort the victims of the man who drove in a busy street like a menace, but also to try to stop him."

655   In Rolf Hochhuth's play *The Deputy* the Pope says, "The Holy See must remain a sanctuary of neutrality."

656   My favorite story about a saint tells how the sturdy Spanish saint, Teresa, riding her mule across scorched Castile, came to a stream in flood. She began to ford it, was swept off her mule into the icy water, and finally staggered, drenched, to the far bank. There she lifted her eyes to heaven: "Is this how you treat your friends, Lord?" The Lord answered "Yes," whereupon Teresa remarked, "No wonder you have so few."

657   The American clergyman John Haynes Holmes once said, "Priests are no more necessary to religion than politicians to patriotism."

658   More timely than ever are the words of Oliver Wendell Holmes, Sr.: "The minister is coming down every generation nearer and nearer to the common level of the useful citizen,—no oracle at all, but a man of more than average moral instincts, who, if he knows anything, knows how little he knows."

659   In the twelfth century the Bishop of Paris wrote to the Pope and asked to be given the assignment of a parish priest. He found the tasks much more arduous than that of bishop. The job of being out with the people administering to their needs was much harder than the paper-shuffling administrative work of the bishop. He wrote back to the Pope, "It is far easier to be a saintly bishop than a godly priest. Demote me and make me bishop again."

660   The late theologian Paul Tillich wrote that three fears have gripped mankind in history. "Before the Christian era it was the fear of death: during the middle ages, fear of guilt. But today it is the fear of meaninglessness. That mad search for escape, for nirvana, for death itself, is the result."

PATRIOTIC SPEAKER

661   Sir Kenneth Clark in his "Civilization" lecture said, "It is the lack of confidence more than anything else that kills a civilization. We can destroy ourselves by cynicism and disillusion, just as effectively as by bombs."

662   Queen Elizabeth II at a Williamsburg dedication ceremony in 1957 said at the Bruton Parish Church, "I want to sit in George Washington's pew." Today, I would like all of you to try to put yourselves back to 1776—to the position of all those Founding Fathers who were ready to risk their fortunes and their lives for independence.

663   In July, 1975, a tourist in Philadelphia asked a cab driver to take him to the old Society Hill section where Independence Hall is. As they were driving up the old streets, the

cab driver remarked, "I sure hope they get rid of these rough old cobblestone streets before all those people come for the Bicentennial.

664   Is Clare Boothe Luce right when she says, "We are coupon clippers on the spiritual investments of our forefathers"?

665   In the winter of 1775 George Washington wrote to his brother John Augustine, "It is my full intention to devote my life and fortune in the cause we are engaged in, if need be."

666   I remember in Maxwell Anderson's play *Valley Forge* when George Washington says to an aide, "This liberty will look easy by and by when nobody dies to get it."

667   When I was last in France I read the inscription at Omaha Beach commemorating the D-Day invasion in 1944: "They endured all, they suffered all—that mankind might know freedom and inherit justice."

668   Former Secretary of HEW, John Gardner, once said: "A nation is never finished. You can't build it and then leave it standing, as the Pharaohs did the Pyramids. It has to be built and rebuilt. It has to be recreated in each generation by believing, caring men and women. It is our turn now. If we don't believe or don't care, nothing can save the nation. If we believe and care, nothing can stop us."

669   General Douglas MacArthur, honoring the American soldiers who fought so bravely in Bataan, said, "And all their yesterdays make possible our tomorrows."

670   There is a famous painting of the signing of the Declaration of Independence which hangs in the White House. It is unusual because for some reason the artist never finished it. Many of the figures in the background of the scene are only sketched in or left blank. That painting reminds us of a profound truth. The American Revolution is unfinished business, with important roles still open for each of us to play.

671   In the 1870s the Ambassador to the Court of St. James's was the poet and writer James Russell Lowell. One day the French historian Guizot, who was also the Ambassador to England, approached Lowell and asked, "Mr. Ambassador, how long will the American republic endure?" Lowell replied, "As long as the ideals of its leaders reflect the ideals of the Founding Fathers."

672   Not too long ago the London *Daily Telegraph* in an editorial told America "to grow up." "For too long," it said, "you have been beating your breasts in self-flagellation in the trauma over Watergate and Vietnam. Too many sections of the press, Congress, TV commentators, comedians, university pundits and a lot of other people think there is a dollar to be made out of denigrating their country's institutions and leaders. It is time you started to remember that you are the leader of the free world."

673   Not long ago this appeared in the *Wall Street Journal:* "Just as the intellectual often sees things the common man misses; so now and then the common man's natural instinct and grass-roots involvement give him insights denied the typical intellectual. And in this case we think the American intellectuals might do well to take a cue from the forgotten American. Not that they should necessarily fly flags, but that they should express in their own style the basic feeling that American society, warts and all, measures up fairly well against actual alternatives. For the common man is on eminently solid ground, we think, in his instinct that what America needs to combat its current 'crisis' is not denigration but affirmation."

674   King Baudouin of Belgium in a visit to this country said in 1959: "America has been called a melting pot, but it seems better to call it a mosaic, for in it each nation, people, or race which has come to its shores has been privileged to keep its individuality, contributing at the same time its share to the unified pattern of a new nation."

675   The late Justice Brandeis once said: "There is in most Americans some spark of idealism, which can be formed into a flame. It takes sometimes a divining rod to find what it is, but when found and . . . when bestowed to the owner, the results are often extraordinary."

676   Justice Lewis Powell said shortly after going on the Supreme Court: "It would be irrational to say that all of the criticisms of America and its institutions are unfounded. Yet excessive self-flagellation is destroying the ties that bind us together."

677   John Gunther once said, "America is the only country deliberately founded on a good idea."

678   The Lord tells the prophet Jeremiah, "Stand by the roads and look and ask for the ancient paths where the good way is and walk in it."

679   I would like to end with the words of the novelist Thomas Wolfe: "I think the true discovery of America is before us. I think the true fulfillment of our spirit, of our people, of our mighty and immortal land, is yet to come."

680   "What then is the American, this new man?" asked the French essayist Michel Guillaume Jean de Crèvecoeur in a small volume of impressions published in 1782. He could only say that the American was a brand-new mixture: "A new man, who acts upon new principles; he must therefore entertain new ideas and form new opinions."

681   In 1893, Katharine Lee Bates wrote in "America the Beautiful" of a "patriot dream that sees beyond the years." In 1960, the poet Archibald MacLeish, debating "national purpose," said: "There are those, I know, who will reply that the liberation of humanity, the freedom of man and mind, is nothing but a dream. They are right. It is. It is the American dream."

682   Theodore Roosevelt said: "We here in America hold in our hands the hope of the world, the fate of the coming years;

and shame and disgrace will be ours if in our eyes the light of high resolve is dimmed, if we trail in the dust the golden hopes of man."

683   As Americans we believe in these principles: We believe in independence, and self-reliance, and in the creative value of the competitive spirit. We believe in full and equal opportunity for all Americans, and in the protection of individual rights and liberties. We believe in the family as the keystone of the community and in the community as the keystone of the nation. We believe in the capacity of people to make their own decisions, in their own lives and in their own communities—and we believe in their right to make those decisions.

684   During the American Revolution, Thomas Paine said, "The cause of America is the cause of all mankind." I think the cause of all mankind is the cause of America. If we succeed here today, the cause of freedom succeeds. If we fail, the cause of freedom fails.

685   In his observations of America, the author Herman Melville wrote: "There is something in the contemplation of the mode in which America has been settled that, in a noble breast, should forever extinguish the prejudices of national dislikes. Settled by the people of all nations, all nations may claim her for their own. You cannot spill a drop of American blood without spilling the blood of the whole world. Be he Englishman, German, Dane, or Scot; the European who scoffs at an American, reviles his own brother, and stands in danger of the judgment. We are not a narrow tribe of men . . . no; our blood is as the flood of the Amazon, made up of a thousand noble currents all pouring into one. We are not a nation so much as a world."

686   In "The Bivouac of the Dead," Theodore O'Hara wrote,

> The muffled drum's sad roll has beat
> The soldier's last tattoo;
> No more on Life's parade shall meet
> The brave and fallen few.

On Fame's eternal camping-ground
　　Their silent tents are spread,
And Glory guards, with solemn round,
　　The bivouac of the dead.

687　　There is an Ashanti proverb which reads, "The ruin of a nation begins in the homes of its people."

688　　Jean Giraudoux in *Electra* writes, "The spirit of a nation is what counts—the look in its eyes."

689　　At a World War I homecoming parade Will Rogers commented, "If they really want to honor the boys, why don't they let them sit in the stands and have the people march by?"

690　　John Adams wrote this letter to his wife on July 3, 1776: "I am well aware of the toil, and blood, and treasure, that it will cost us to maintain this declaration, and support and defend these States. Yet, through all the gloom, I can see the rays of ravishing light and glory. . . . The second day of July, 1776, will be the most memorable epoch in the history of America. I am apt to believe that it will be celebrated by succeeding generations as the great anniversary festival. It ought to be commemorated as the day of deliverance, by solemn acts of devotion to God Almighty. It ought to be solemnized with pomp and parade, with shows, games, sports, guns, bells, bonfires, and illuminations, from one end of this continent to the other, from this time forward for evermore."

691　　As John Adams wrote to his wife, "Posterity! You will never know how much it cost the present generation to preserve your freedom! I hope you will make a good use of it. If you do not, I shall repent it in heaven that I ever took half the pains to preserve it."

692　　In Leo Tolstoy's *War and Peace,* Prince Andrei's comments on Austerlitz were, "We lost because we told ourselves we lost."

693   The Lutheran minister Peter Muhlenberg in the beginning of the Revolutionary War had mixed feelings about clergymen fighting in a war. In January, 1776, he resolved those feelings in a dramatic sermon to his congregation. Tearing off his black clerical garb to show a blue continental army uniform, he stepped down from the pulpit, saying, "There is a time to preach and a time to pray but there is also a time to fight and that time has come."

694   In August of 1865 when Benjamin and Mrs. Disraeli paid a visit to Raby Castle, home of the Duke and Duchess of Cleveland, their son Lord Rosebery was charmed by the brilliant leader of the Conservative party. After they left, Rosebery looked into the visitors' book where the names of the guests and their professions were recorded. It said:

> NAME: B. DISRAELI
> PROFESSION: PATRIOTISM

695   President Herbert Hoover made the following speech at Valley Forge, February, 1931, and repeated it again in February, 1958:

The nation is beset with difficulties and confusions. Many of us have doubt and grave concern for the future. But no one who reviews the past and realizes the vast strength of our people can doubt that this, like a score of similar experiences in our history, is a passing trial. From this knowledge must come the courage and wisdom to improve and strengthen us for the future.

We must not be misled by the claim that the source of all wisdom is in the government. Wisdom is born out of experience, and most of all out of precisely such experience as is brought to us by the darkest moments. It is in the meeting of such moments that are born new insights, new sympathies, new powers, new skills.

Such conflicts as we are in the midst of today cannot be won by any single stroke, by any one strategy sprung from the mind of any single genius. Rather must we pin our faith upon the inventiveness, the resourcefulness, the initiative of every one of us. That cannot fail us if we keep faith in ourselves and our future, and in the constant growth of our intelligence and ability to cooperate with one another.

The memory of Americans who glory in Valley Forge tells us the truth which echoes upward from this soil of blood and tears: The way to greatness is the path of self-reliance, independence, and steadfastness in time of trial and stress.

696   This sovereign faith of ours in the freedom and dignity of the individual is infinitely more than a dry and lifeless philosophic doctrine. It is the nerve and the fiber of our very laws.

This sovereign ideal we believe to be the very source of greatness and the genius of America.

In this, we proclaim nothing very new. It was seen clearly by a wise French visitor, De Tocqueville, who came to America considerably more than a century ago. He patiently sought the greatness and genius of America in our fields and in our forests, in our mines and in our commerce, in our Congress and in our Constitution, and he found them not. But he sought further and then he said: "Not until I went into the churches of America and her pulpits aflame with righteousness did I understand the secret of her genius and power. America is great because America is good—and if America ever ceases to be good—America will cease to be great."

697   We all know how the Declaration of Independence begins, but do we know how it ends? Do we know what was the last sentence after which they signed their names in that July of 1776? Our founding fathers committed all of themselves. These are the last words: "And for the support of this declaration, with a firm Reliance on the Protection of divine Providence, we mutually pledge to each other our lives, our Fortunes, and our sacred Honor."

698   Massachusetts chose the young John Adams to be its delegate to the Second Continental Congress. They were to meet to plan how their grievances could be redressed. But a resolution of independence was adopted and the young Adams was elected to be on the committee of three with Franklin and Jefferson to draft a document.

When Jefferson's draft was challenged and criticized by some of the delegates, Adams rose and appealed to the Congress: "Sink or swim, live or die, survive or perish, I give my hand and my heart to this vote. Sir, before God, I believe that the hour has come. . . . My whole heart is in this measure, all that I have, all that I am, all that I hope in this life. I am now ready here to stake upon it."

699   Charles Evans Hughes, former Chief Justice of the United States Supreme Court, once said in a speech about the flag: "You cannot be saved by valor and devotion to your ancestors. To each generation comes its patriotic duty, and upon your willingness to sacrifice and endure, as those before you have sacrificed and endured, rests the national hope."

700   Benjamin Franklin's *Gazette* rejoiced editorially when the General Assembly of Pennsylvania, in March, 1729, appropriated two thousand pounds for the erection of a State House at Fourth and Chestnut. Twenty years later, Franklin himself was a member of the General Assembly when it ordered from the Robert Charles firm of London a bell to be cast. Franklin was a member of that Assembly when it selected, as the inscription for the lip of the bell, the passage from Leviticus 25:10: "Proclaim liberty throughout all the land unto all the inhabitants thereof."

The bell, brought over in the *Matilda* by Captain Budden, was mounted in the State House in August, 1752. But, twenty-four years later, the prophetic message was to ring out to all the world.

It was the destiny of Benjamin Franklin to play a part in the fulfillment of this inscription on July 4, 1776. Franklin made freedom ring in his life. Let each of us give meaning to that inscription.

701   At the end of the Revolutionary War the Commander of the Continental Armies, George Washington, wrote a letter to the governors who had now become the chief executives of the thirteen new states. "I now make it my earnest prayer that God would have you and the state over which you preside in

his holy protection. That He would graciously be pleased to dispose us all to do justice, to love mercy, and to demean ourselves with charity and humility, and a pacific temper of mind, which were characteristics of the divine author of our blessed religion, and without an humble imitation of whose example in these things, we can never hope to be a happy nation."

PHILOSOPHER

702   Centuries ago Socrates told us, "The shortest way to live with honor is to strive to be what you would like to have others think you are."

703   It is noteworthy that Sir Kenneth Clark concluded his remarkable film series on civilization with his own credo: "At this point, I reveal myself in my true colors, as a stick-in-the-mud. I believe that order is better than chaos, creation better than destruction. I prefer gentleness to violence, forgiveness to vendetta. On the whole I think that knowledge is better than ignorance, and I am sure that human sympathy is better than ideology. I believe that in spite of the recent triumphs of science, men haven't changed much in the last two thousand years; and in consequence we must still try to learn from history. . . . Above all, I believe in the God-given genius of certain individuals and I value a society that makes their existence possible."

704   A young man asked Dr. William Menninger the question of how to achieve mental health. Dr. Menninger replied, "Find a mission in life and take it seriously."

705   José Ortega y Gasset said, "Life is a series of collisions with the future; it is not a sum of what we have been but what we yearn to be."

706   Samuel Butler once said that "life is like playing a violin solo in public and learning the instrument as one goes on."

707   In Jason Miller's play *That Championship Season,* Daley, the junior high school principal, cries out, "I'm being swallowed up by my own anonymity."

708   In *Two Cheers for Democracy* E. M. Forster wrote: "Tolerance is a very dull virtue. It is boring. Unlike love, it has always had a bad press. No one has ever written an ode to tolerance or raised a statue to her. Yet this is the quality which will be most needed. . . . This is the sound state of mind which we are looking for. This is the only force which will enable different races and classes and interests to settle down together."

709   As Albert Camus put it, "Without work all life goes rotten. But when work is soulless, life stifles and dies."

710   Dr. Elton Trueblood, Quaker author and philosopher, wrote some years ago: "The decline of laughter appears to depend on nothing more profound than the recognition that ours is an imperfect world. Why this should be a shocking discovery, I have no idea, but it seems to be such to many in our generation. Much of the problem is really philosophical. Millions have imbibed the sentimental idea of natural human goodness and have really expected Utopia right around the corner. When it does not come, they are angry in their disappointment and begin to indulge in harsh judgment of others. The emphasis, accordingly, is always on other people's sins, but never on our own. If only the establishment could be changed or replaced, then the problem would be solved! But, of course, it is not solved. In the progress of the French Revolution the establishment was displaced, all right, but what ensued was a reign of terror."

711   John Gardner, the former Secretary of Health, Education and Welfare, recently observed that America was raising a generation of managers but not leaders—and that the managers were becoming so specialized in one aspect of the larger operation that they had no time, energy, or eventually capacity to see the larger purposes of what they were doing."

712   Theodore Roosevelt once said that the best prize life offers is the chance to work at work worth doing.

713   The distinguished Britisher Alistair Cooke said recently that he visited an American home that seemed to have everything; two cars in the garage, a beautiful living room with expensive furniture, a color TV set, a kitchen filled with the latest gadgets, and a large pool and beautiful patio. However, the lady of the house was reading a book entitled *How to Be Happy.*

714   I remember something that Sir Winston Churchill, the man whose courage, faith, and persistence carried his nation through the darkest days of World War II, said. The headmaster of the prep school Sir Winston had attended when he was a boy asked him to speak to the students. The headmaster told the boys to have their pencils and pads ready and take down whatever he said. The moment came for him to speak. The old warrior rose to his feet and spoke these words, "Never give in. Never give in. Never, never, never, never, never give in!" And he sat down. Don't let anything defeat you.

715   In *Random Harvest,* James Hilton, wrote: "Life's more important than a living. So many people who make a living are making death, not life. Don't ever join them. They're the gravediggers of our civilization—the safe men, the compromisers, the money-makers, the muddlers-through."

716   Christopher Morley wrote: "There are fashions in saying things just as there are fashions in clothes. You wear what other people are wearing not so much because it's attractive but so as not to be conspicuous; so you can go on being yourself underneath, without being noticed too much. Except by the people you want to be noticed by."

717   In Willa Cather's *Death Comes for the Archbishop* the bishop says to the priest, "I shall not die of a cold, my son. I shall die of having lived."

718   Some years ago a University of Pennsylvania professor of psychiatry, Dr. Earl Bond, estimated that one out of 140 Americans is perfect—that means no anxieties, no fears, no prejudices, no vices, and no weaknesses. But, says Dr. Bond, "you won't envy them—they are perfectly well-rounded and equal—like a string of zeroes.

719   Henry David Thoreau once wrote, "It is not enough to be busy . . . the question is: What are we busy about?"

720   Rabbi Hillel, the famous Jewish scholar, said, "If I am not for myself, who will be for me?" "But," he continued, "if I am only for myself, what am I? If not now, when?" The message being that we must stand up not only for ourselves, but others as well.

721   A newspaperman once asked Justice Oliver Wendell Holmes on his nintieth birthday, "What's the secret of your success, Justice Holmes?" "Young man," replied Holmes, "the secret of my success is that very early I discovered that I'm not God."

722   The novelist John O'Hara wrote in a letter: "I have a theological theory that God is, among other things, the Supreme Ironist, that no matter how long or short a time you spend in this life, it all evens up in the end."

723   "Our youths love luxury. They have bad manners, contempt for authority, they show disrespect for their elders, and have to chatter in place of exercise. Children are now tyrants, not the servants to their households. They no longer rise when their elders enter the room. They contradict their parents, chatter before company, gobble up their food, and tyrannize their teachers." If you think this is a description of modern America, you're wrong—Plato reports Socrates saying this, four centuries before Christ.

724   During these times I am reminded of what the philosopher George Santayana said: "Life is not a spectacle or a feast; it is a predicament."

725   The Spanish philosopher José Ortega y Gasset once said, "Life cannot wait until the sciences may have explained the universe scientifically. We cannot put off living until we are ready. The most salient characteristic of life is its coerciveness: it is always urgent, 'here and now' without any possible postponement. Life is fired at us point blank."

726   Horace Walpole once described the world as "a comedy to those who think and a tragedy to those who feel."

727   The English historian Arnold Toynbee once remarked that "civilization is a movement and not a condition, a voyage and not a harbor."

PHYSICIAN

728   Doctor Benjamin Rush, the signer of the Declaration of Independence as well as being the first doctor to establish a free medical clinic in the U.S., composed his own epitaph, which read, "I was an advocate of principles in medicine." Today I would like to discuss some of those principles which we have for so long taken for granted.

- Hippocratic oath—euthanasia
- • Helping all in need—malpractice insurance walkout
- • • Responsibility to community—socialized medicine

729   The English philosopher Lord Bryce once wrote that Medicine is "the only profession that labors incessantly to destroy the reason for its own existence." It is that quality which makes us one of the most honored professions—and that is why the accusation that we promote operations is the most devastating charge . . .

730   The highest-paid doctor in all history was Jacques Corteau, who was paid almost five million a year along with eight castles for keeping King Louis XI of France healthy.

731   The Canadian doctor Sir William Osler once had good advice for the medical practitioner: "The great physician cares more about the individual patient than for the special nature of the disease." Osler meant we should know more about the patient than just his physical symptoms—his emotional stress, his worries. All these are part of the whole man that must be treated.

732   When Dr. Jonas Salk received a medal from President Eisenhower in 1956 for discovering the polio vaccine, he said, "I feel the greatest regard for doing is the opportunity to do more." Similarly, the highest satisfaction in being a doctor is seeing the sick become healthy, the diseased cured—of being needed—of being God's instrument of healing.

733   In Imperial China doctors were paid as long as the patients remained healthy. Naturally it was in the doctor's own interest that a patient's illness should last as short a time as possible. While no one suggests that type of compensation, certainly the idea of preventive medicine is an idea whose time has come.

734   Benjamin Franklin was right when he said, "God cures and the doctor takes the fee." Today doctors can overprescribe and overreact. But sometimes nature can be the best cure.

735   Dr. Oliver Wendell Holmes, Sr., before he became a writer, was a practicing physician. Some of his patients questioned whether he was a very serious doctor because, for a while, he had a sign posted in his office that read, "Small fevers gratefully received."

736   St. Luke, "the beloved physician" of the New Testament, records Christ saying, "Of those to whom much is given, much is required."

737   James Smithson, the founder of the Smithsonian Institution, was suffering from a disease no doctor could diagnose. "I hope," he said at one point to one doctor, "that you perform an autopsy to discover what is the matter with me, for I am dying to know what my ailment is."

738   In Ionesco's *Hippotamus* the character Daisy tells her friend Berenger, "Doctors invent illnesses." "Yes," he replies, "but they do it in good faith."

PLAYBOY

739   I remember the lines of the Justice to Falstaff in *Henry IV:* "Your means are very slender, and your waste is great." And Falstaff replied, patting his girth, "I would my means were greater and my waist slenderer."

740   I like the way Bronson Alcott was once described: "He soared to the infinite and dived into the unfathomable, but never paid cash."

741   James Thurber said, "We all have flaws and mine is . being wicked."

POLICE OFFICIAL

742   The historian and philosopher Will Durant wrote, "Eternal vigilance is the price of order as well as liberty." Today community groups can help keep peace and order in their neighborhoods.

743   In Roman times Seneca said, "He who does not report a crime or help prevent it, encourages it."

744   In one of his first letters as President, George Washington wrote to his Attorney General Edmund Randolph, saying the administration of justice is the finest pillar of government. The question today is how to improve the administration of justice.

> • Up-grade police
> •• Jail sentencings
> ••• Criminal-court process

745   In his *City of God* Saint Augustine asks, "If justice is taken away, then what is the Kingdom, but a great robbery? For what are robberies themselves but little Kingdoms?" Today the lawless jungles in some of our big cities are anarchy.

746   In the last line of the Book of Judges, it is written that there was no ruler, no magistrate, and each man did what was right in his own eyes. We cannot have justice unless we have the rule of law—which means no one, not even a judge or a president, stands above the law.

747   Eric Sevareid said, "It is not our freedom that is in jeopardy, in the first instance; it is our public order. If that breaks down, freedom will be lost and so . . . will the prospect for greater justice."

748   Walter Lippmann said, "The balance of power within our society has turned dangerously against the peace forces." Today I want to discuss some of the recent court decisions and how they have hampered criminal investigation and prosecution.

749   Abraham Lincoln said, "Too much reliance is placed in noisy demonstrations—they excite prejudice and close the avenues to sober reason." The right of assembly does not mean the right of mob demonstrations that trespass on individual rights.

750   In the Gilbert and Sullivan ditty the policeman sings:

> When constabulary's duty's to be done
> A policeman's lot is not a happy one.

POLITICIAN

751   In a recent study of public attitudes towards twenty major occupations, physicians and clergymen were first and

second. Politicians and used-car salesmen were nineteenth and twentieth.

752   There are those such as Walter Lippmann who believe the art of politics is to accommodate the demands of favor seekers on the one hand and to soothe the rest of the public with noble sentiments and patriotic phrases. But tonight I would like to offer some cold and harsh facts about a controversial problem.

753   The American dream may still be that mothers like to think their sons could grow up to be President, but according to a famous Gallup poll of some years ago, some 86 percent do not want them to become politicians.

754   The philosopher Will Durant wrote: "All politics is the rivalry of organized minorities; the voters are the bleachers who cheer the victors and jeer the defeats but do not otherwise contribute to the result." Well, an organized minority is prevailing in their pressure . . .

755   It might be useful to recall what Speaker Sam Rayburn used to say to every freshman class of Democratic Congressmen: "Boys, just remember, you can never be defeated because of something you don't say."

756   In politics there is always pressure to follow the Pickwickian rule. You will recall in Dickens the words of Mr. Pickwick, "It's always best on these occasions to do what the mob do." "But," said Mr. Snodgrass, "suppose there are two mobs?" "Shout with the largest," replied Mr. Pickwick.

757   Only Churchill had the right words to describe the present administration. "No government," he once said, "has ever combined so passionate a lust for power with such incurable impotence in its exercise."

758   Before I make the following proposal, I want to quote the traditional advice given to a freshman member of the House of Commons: "If you want to make a success the first

time you speak, deliver a general panegyric on economy; if you want to invite failure, propose a particular item that should be cut."

759   As Mayor La Guardia said, "I don't believe there's a Republican way to clean streets or for that matter a Democratic way to run a government. There's just a right way and a wrong way."

760   I realize it takes no courage for a politician to take issue with Lenin. But I think it instructive to remind ourselves that it was Lenin who said the best way to crush the middle class is to grind them between the millstones of taxation and inflation.

761   I am not an idealogue of either left or right. I agree with Alexander Pope, who said:

> For forms of government let fools contest
> What-e'er is best administered is best.

762   I am not ashamed to be a politician. As Harry Truman once said, "A politician is a man who understands government, and it takes a politician to run a government. A statesman is just a politician who's been dead ten or fifteen years."

763   The Senator reminds me of that character in George Higgins's book *A City on the Hill.* He was described as a man who really yearned to be a philanthropist, but since he wasn't rich he did the next best thing—ran for Congress to give away the public money.

764   In one of O. Henry's short stories a political character says, "A straw vote only shows which way the hot air blows."

POPULATION PLANNER

765   There is an old Arab saying that a man must do three things in life: plant trees, write books, and have sons. Well, I wish they would plant more trees and write more books.

PRESS

766   McCandlish Phillips, a veteran *New York Times* reporter, used to say he'd start a small journalism school in Manhattan. Each day the students would gather at the door and if it was not raining or snowing the professor would stand on the roof pouring buckets of water onto the class. Then at five o'clock the professor would run downstairs, open the door from the inside, poke out his head and say, "No comment."

PROFESSOR

767   As Adlai Stevenson expressed it, "A professor is just a man who takes more words than necessary to tell more than he knows."

768   How did John Kenneth Galbraith describe the academic? "A professor is just another name for pedagogue, and a pedagogue is just a demagogue with a Ph.D."

769   The English poet W. H. Auden called a professor one who talks in someone else's sleep.

770   Dr. Nicholas Murray Butler, president of Columbia University, said that "an academic expert is one who knows more and more about less and less."

PROPHET

771   A Greek dramatist said a prophet is one who guesses well.

772   As Shakespeare said,

> If you can look into the seeds of time
> And say which grain will grow and which will not,
> Speak then to me.

773   Lord Byron once penned these words about the prophet who makes the mistake of being right:

> Of all the horrid, hideous notes of woe . . .
> Is that portentous phrase, "I told you so."

PROSECUTOR

774   In *The People, Yes* Carl Sandburg wrote: "Revolt and Terror pay a price. Order and law have a cost." Sandburg knew that liberty unless balanced by law is license and that democracy without order is anarchy.

PTA PRESIDENT

775   Some months ago I overheard a family in a restaurant. The waitress asked a boy, "What will you have, sonny?" The boy said shyly, "I want a hot dog." Before the waitress could write down the order the mother interrupted, "No hot dog," she said. "Give him potatoes, beef and carrots." But the waitress ignored her completely. "Do you want ketchup or mustard on your hot dog?" she asked of the boy. "Ketchup," he replied with a happy smile on his face. "Coming up," the waitress said, starting for the kitchen. There was a stunned silence upon her departure. Finally, the boy turned to his parents. "Know what?" he said. "She thinks I'm real."

776   A graduate student working on juvenile delinquency reported in a Wisconsin sociology seminar difficulty in collecting data. He had phoned a dozen homes around 9 P.M. and asked parents if they knew where their children were at that hour. "My first few calls," he reported, "were answered by children who had no idea where their parents were."

777   As John Mason Brown said, "Reasoning with a child is fine, if you can reach the child's reason without losing your own."

778   George Bernard Shaw once advised: "If you must hold yourself up to your children as an object lesson, hold yourself up as a warning and not as an example."

779   Oscar Wilde wrote, "Children begin by loving their parents. After a time they judge them. Rarely, if ever, do they forgive them."

PUBLIC OFFICIAL

780   C. Northcote Parkinson never penned a better paper-work-jungle story than the recently-published Senate Government Operations Committee report listing the Federal Government's 1,242 advisory boards, commissions and councils, as well as naming the 22,702 persons who hold positions on at least one of them. The horror of the book—like the horror of the bureaucracy it catalogs—lies in its enormous size. The index is a painful 1,412 pages long.

781   There are those who claim ours is a "sick" society; that our country is sick; our government is sick; that we are sick. Well, maybe they're right. I submit that I'm sick. . . . I am sick of commentators and columnists canonizing anarchists, revolutionaries, and criminal rapists, but condemning law enforcement when such criminals are brought to justice. I am sick of Supreme Court decisions which turn criminals loose on society —while other decisions try to take away my means of protecting my home and family. I am sick of being told that policemen are mad dogs who should not have guns—but that criminals who use guns to rob, maim, and murder should be understood and helped back to society.

782   I am reminded of the time a cabinet aide came to President Taft at the outset of his administration to brief him on what he called "the machinery of government." When he left, Taft remarked to a friend, "You know—that poor fellow really thinks it is machinery and not people." Government is not machinery—it is people responding to people.

783 Benjamin Franklin once said, "I shall never ask, never refuse, nor ever resign an office."

784 Winston Churchill once said, "Among the deficiencies of hindsight is that while we know the consequences of what was done, we do not know the consequences of some other course that was not followed."

785 Adlai Stevenson once expressed this truth about government: "Bad administration can destroy good policy but good administration can never save bad policy."

786 I know a lot of people today agree that public office is "the last refuge of a scoundrel."

787 Brooks Atkinson once remarked that "the perfect bureaucrat everywhere is the man who manages to make no decisions and escape all responsibility."

788 Too many officials learn only how to strut sitting down.

789 Lyndon B. Johnson once remarked: "The Secretary of Labor is in charge of finding you a job, the Secretary of the Treasury is in charge of taking half the money you make away from you, and the Attorney General is in charge of suing you for the other half."

790 The first governor of the Massachusetts Bay Colony John Winthrop addressed his shipmates on the *Arbella:* "We must always consider that we shall be as a city upon a hill—the eyes of all people upon us."

791 As the French Premier Clemenceau wrote, "There is no passion like that of the *fonctionnaire* for his function."

SAILOR

792 Dr. Samuel Johnson once said, "No man will be a sailor who has contrivance enough to get himself into a jail; for being in a ship is being in a jail, with the chance of being drowned.

. . . A man in jail has more room, better food, and commonly better company."

SALESMAN

793   The British publisher Lord Thomson wrote that the difference between rape and ecstasy is salesmanship.

794   What's that line from *The Music Man?* "You've got to know the territory,"? Well, that's so right—one must study the territory.

795   Some years ago a shoe manufacturer sent two salesmen into interior Africa. The first salesman wired back, "Situation impossible. No one wears shoes." But the second one wired back, "No one wears shoes—opportunities unlimited."

SCIENTIST

796   Henry Miller once wrote, "The wallpaper with which men of science have covered the world of reality is falling to tatters." In recent years science has discovered how much we don't know.

797   The poet Lord Tennyson once wrote, "Science moves, but slowly, slowly creeping on from point to point." Medical science has not discovered the cure for cancer but progress in research has been made from point to point. Tonight I would like to list some of the breakthroughs.

798   The French writer Valéry wrote, "Science is a collection of successful recipes." One technique perfected . . .

799   C. P. Snow, British author and scientist, who is appalled at the illiteracy of liberal-arts people, often asks them if they can describe the Second Law of Thermodynamics. Their response is usually negative. "Yet," says Snow, "that is about the scientific equivalent of 'Have you read a work of Shake-

speare's?'" Tonight I would like to talk about the need for scientific education.

800   Dr. Milton Eisenhower once wrote, "Modern man worships at the temple of science, but science tells him only what is possible, not what is right."

801   When the distinguished British scientist Thomas Huxley came to America, he visited Johns Hopkins University in Baltimore. He was asked if he was impressed with America's industrial power and developing technology. "Yes," said Dr. Huxley, "it has great potential, but what are you going to do with it?"

802   Michael Faraday once exhibited the dynamo to British Prime Minister Disraeli. Disraeli looked at the forerunner of all generators and said, "What good is that?" And Faraday replied, "What good is a baby, Mr. Disraeli?" Tonight I would like to talk about the meaning of a new scientific development.

803   Adlai Stevenson once observed, "Man has wrested from nature the power to make the world a desert and to make the deserts bloom. There is no evil in the atom; only in men's souls."

804   Dr. Lincoln Barnett once wrote, "The quick harvest of applied science is the usable process, the medicine, the machine. The shy fruit of pure science is Understanding."

805   "Science," said Dr. Oliver Wendell Holmes, Sr., "is a first-rate piece of furniture for a man's upper chamber, if he has common sense on the ground floor."

806   Dr. Glenn Seaborg once said: "People must understand that science is inherently neither a potential for good nor for evil. It is a potential to be harnessed by man to do his bidding."

807   T. H. Huxley once wrote the scientist's prayer, "Lord —give me the strength to face a fact though it slay me."

808   Not long ago a little girl was asked by her teacher to name some of Thomas Edison's contributions to science. She answered, "If it weren't for Edison, we'd all still be watching television by candlelight."

809   When Thomas Edison was trying without success to find a suitable filament for an incandescent light bulb, a sympathetic friend asked if it wasn't depressing to work so hard without making any discoveries. "Not at all," Edison replied. "I've already discovered eighty-seven filaments that don't work."

810   Walter Bagehot, the British economist, once said of scientists: "Some people are unfortunately born scientific— they have skill in fishes and attain renown in pebbles—there is a coldness to their fame."

811   On July 22, 1962, Mariner I failed to achieve its orbital goal. In the coded instructions a hyphen was misplaced, causing the launch vehicle to vibrate, with the result that the launch vehicle along with its payload—Mariner I—changed its course and ended up in the Atlantic Ocean and had to be destroyed at a cost of $40 million.

812   Isaac Newton wrote in his diary: "I seem to have been only like a boy playing on the seashore . . . whilst the great ocean of truth lay all undiscovered before me."

813   The scientist Thomas Huxley once described a disaster as "an induction killed by a fact."

814   It was Dr. Albert Einstein who said, "Just when humanity found the means to overcome its problems, it forgot what they were, and lost its purpose."

815   Charles Steinmetz, the great scientist, was once asked which field for future research offered the greatest promise. "Prayer," he replied instantly. "Find out about prayer."

816   The great scientist Louis Pasteur once said, "Let me tell you the secret that has led me to my goal. My strength lies solely in my tenacity."

817   J. Robert Oppenheimer after the first atomic test said, "We knew the world would not be the same."

818   In 1970, papers were written to rationalize the moon landing. They said, "It was a mirage—the television was done by trick photography and mirrors."

819   Thomas Huxley, the English scientist and philosopher, visited America a hundred years ago. At the opening of Johns Hopkins University he was asked to predict the future destiny of America: "I cannot say that I am in the slightest degree impressed by your bigness or your material resources. Size is not grandeur and territory does not make a nation. The great issue about which hangs a true sublimity and the terror of over-hanging fate, is what are you going to do with all these things? What is to be the end to which these are to be the means?"

820   The great French scientist Louis Pasteur reached the height of his career when at the young age of thirty-two he became a professor and dean of the newly formed Faculty of Science in the then recently established University of Lille. At his inaugural lecture a mass assemblage of students, scientists, and professors were waiting. At the close of his speech he mentioned that a new era of prosperity was about to blossom for the Faculty of Science in chemistry, electricity, and physics. He called on the young people to answer this call to the service of mankind and spoke of the challenge and contributions that awaited their enlistment. He said that training must be afforded to match this idealism of the French youth. To them he said, "Chance favors only those minds which are prepared."

SENIOR CITIZEN

821   In one of Graham Greene's novels, a doctor says to an architect, "One never retires from a vocation."

822   When people ask me how I feel these days, I say what Somerset Maugham said on his ninetieth birthday, "Not bad when you consider the alternative."

823   As Bernard Baruch once said, "Old age is always fifteen years older than I am."

824   It is said that the denunciation of the young is a necessary part of the hygiene of older people and greatly assists the circulation of their blood. But tonight I would like to praise what some young people . . .

825   When cabinet member Walter Hickel left office he said, "I left a living and found a life."

826   On his ninetieth Birthday Bernard Baruch was asked what was the most important lesson he had learned during his life. Baruch replied, "Mind my own business."

827   When P. T. Barnum was near death the *Evening Sun* of New York asked the great showman's publicity agent if Barnum would object to having his obituary published before he died. The agent said, "The old man will be delighted." The next day Barnum read four columns about his own death and he loved it. And after the presentation this evening I feel like I just heard my own obituary.

828   In "De Gustibus" Robert Browning wrote: Open my heart and you will see/Graved inside of it, 'Italy'. And open my heart you will find engraved on it . . .

829   In La Granja, Spain, palace officials built a stairway around a tree so that King Philip V at the age of sixty could climb the favorite tree of his childhood. Tonight I would like to relive one of my favorite childhood memories.

830   When John Jay, one of the Founding Fathers, was asked how it was possible for him to occupy his mind after his retirement from public life, he said, "I have a long life to look back upon and an eternity to look forward to."

831   I may be hard to convince to retire. But I am not nearly as hard to convince as my grandaughter at bedtime.

832   Most people say that as you get old you have to give up things. I think you get old because you give up things.

833   It was John Barrymore who said, "A man is not old until regrets take the place of dreams."

834   As George Bernard Shaw said, "At my age you are neither well nor dead."

835   Benjamin Disraeli said when man fades into his anecdotage it is time to retire. I guess now that I am retiring I can begin some anecdotage.

836   When the old Roman Cato began to study Greek at the age of eighty, a friend asked him why he was starting out on so large a task at such an advanced age. Cato answered that it was the youngest age he had left.

837   I am so often reminded of the words of Bernard Baruch: "An elder statesman is somebody old enough to know his own mind and keep quiet about it."

838   In 1780 Benjamin Franklin wrote this letter of retirement to George Washington: "I must soon quit the scene, but you may live to see our Country flourish, as it will amazingly and rapidly after the War is over. Like a field of young Indian corn, which long fair weather and sunshine had enfeebled and discolored, and which in that weak state, by a thunder gust, of violent wind, hail, and rain, seem'd to be threaten'd with absolute destruction; yet the storm being past, it recovers fresh verdure, shoots up with double vigour, and delights the eye, not of its owner only, but of every observing traveller."

839   A character without a name in Ionesco's novel *The Hermit* says, "I'd consider resigning but I didn't know what to resign myself to."

840   One of Adlai Stevenson's favorite stories was about a man who was 102 years old. He was being interviewed on his birthday and was asked what he attributed his long life to. He said he had never smoked, drunk, nor overloaded his

stomach. He went to bed early and got up early. The reporter said, "You know, I had an uncle who did the same things, but he lived to be only 89. What do you attribute that to?" The old man replied, "He just didn't keep it up long enough."

841   Once when contemplating old age Oliver Wendell Holmes said, "The young man knows the rules but the old man knows the exceptions."

842   General Charles de Gaulle once said, "Old age is a shipwreck."

843   Charlie Conerly of the New York Giants once said, "When you win, you're an old pro. When you lose you're an old man."

844   I close by quoting what Shakespeare's Wolsey said:

> Farewell, a long farewell, to all my greatness!
> This is the state of man: to-day he puts forth
> The tender leaves of hope; tomorrow blossoms
> And bears his blushing honors thick upon him;
> The third day comes a frost, a killing frost,
> And when he thinks, good easy man, full surely
> His greatness is a-ripening, nips his root,
> And then he falls, as I do.

845   Reflecting on old age Francis Cardinal Spellman said, "You've heard of the three ages of man—youth, maturity, and 'You are looking wonderful.' "

846   Senator Claiborne Pell said, "People only leave by way of the box—ballot or coffin."

SOCIAL WORKER

847   Count Leo Tolstoy wrote in *Anna Karenina,* "All happy families resemble one another, every unhappy family is unhappy in its own way." It might be poverty, sickness, marital

discord, and a worker must be able to assess medical, legal, or psychological needs.

848   In Bob Dylan's song *Blowin' in the Wind* the words go, "How many ears must one man have before he can hear people cry."

849   As the prophet Isaiah counseled, "He shall not judge by what his eyes see or decide by what his ears hear but with righteousness he shall aid those in need and decide with equity for the weak of the earth."

SOCIOLOGIST

850   Recently I read a statement which read, "The earth is degenerating these days. Bribery and corruption abound. Children no longer mind parents. Every man wants to write a book and it is evident that the end of the world is approaching fast." That came from an Assyrian tablet written in 3000 B.C.

851   In Ionesco's *The Bald Soprano* a character commuting on a train to New York finds that his companion also lives in New Haven, and that she also has a seven-year-old daughter— they find out they live in the same house and are married.

852   Donald Swann, the actor, tells about the Indian man he sat next to on a flight from Hawaii to Bombay. The man was completely bewildered by the breakfast served by the Pan American stewardess. First, he poured his coffee into the cornflakes and ate them. Then he mixed the milk and sugar and drank it. Next he licked the butter from the small square of waxed paper. Finally, he tried to drink the marmalade.

SOLDIER

853   George Washington once penned his creed as a soldier to his Secretary of War, Henry Knox: "Integrity and firmness is all I promise. These shall never forsake me, although I may be

deserted by all men." Our speaker today exemplified such resolution . . .

854   Some may think the role of a career soldier is still Gilbert and Sullivan:

> I am the very pattern of a modern major-general
> I've information vegetable, animal and mineral
> I know the Kings of England and I quote the fights historical
> From Marathon to Waterloo, in order categorical.

But in our modern service memorizing old battles is least important as a qualification—today it is the art of public administration, political science, computer technology . . .

855   In Plutarch's *Lives* an Athenian General is quoted: "In war there is no room for two mistakes." Today I would like to outline at least two mistakes that have been made in our defense program.

856   It was a lieutenant with Cromwell who said, "On becoming soldiers, we have not ceased to be citizens."

857   It was George Bernard Shaw who wrote, "A soldier is an anachronism." And I suppose since Vietnam many social critics would agree with that estimate. But if the professional soldier is out of date who will hold the shield that allows our peacetime nation to live and grow?

858   As Shakespeare said,

> 'Tis the soldiers' life
> To have their balcony slumbers waked with strife.

The bard might have been writing about the Reserves.

859   Napoleon wrote that even more important than courage was the ability to withstand being tired and bored.

860   George Washington said, "To be prepared for war is one of the most effective means of preserving peace."

861   Remember what Kipling said of the career soldier:

> It's Tommy this, an' Tommy that, an'
> "Chuck 'im out, the brute!"
> But it's "Savior of 'is country," when
> the guns begin to shoot.

862   In an old sentry box in Gibraltar there is carved this ditty:

> God and the soldier all men adore
> In time of trouble and no more
> For when war is over and all things righted
> God is neglected and the soldier slighted.

863   As Napoleon said, "Soldiers win battles but generals get the credit."

864   Perhaps I should have followed the advice of Omar Bradley, who said, "The best service a retired general can perform is to turn in his tongue along with his uniform."

865   In the Constitutional Convention a delegate suggested that a clause should forbid more than a five thousand-man standing army. "Fine," said George Washington, "and the next clause should forbid any enemy from attacking us with more than five thousand men."

866   Omar Bradley said, "We have become nuclear giants but ethical infants. We know more about killing than we know about living."

867   Lord Cecil once advised his sovereign, Queen Elizabeth: "Soldiers in peace are like chimneys in summer."

868   I remember a latrine sign in World War II in Fort Benning. It read:

> Soldiers who wish to be a hero
> Are practically zero.
> But those who wish to be civilians,
> Jesus, they run into millions.

869   When a writer to the London *Times* sneered that lords were bred only for the battlefield and the boudoir, Lord Clifford of Chudleigh replied, "The attributes which come with both of these pursuits—diplomacy, tactics, courage and good earthy realism—are surely of some use to the nation."

SPORTS FIGURE

870   I remember what Branch Rickey told a fellow club owner when he proposed to break the color line by hiring Jackie Robinson, "I want to make major league baseball an all-American game." Well, Little League today is more than an all-American game. It is an all-world game with thirty-two countries involved.

871   Vince Lombardi said, "Winning isn't the best thing, it is the only thing." Well, maybe that isn't always true but as they say about money, "It isn't the only thing but it'll do till something better comes along."

872   Former middleweight champion Sugar Ray Robinson was asked what made him turn to boxing. Robinson said, "Well, I looked at these two hands one day and neither of them had any money in it."

873   John Unitas, the great professional football quarterback explained why he decided to stop playing football. "I could have played two or three more seasons. All I needed was a leg transplant." But at the rate I was going I needed more than just a leg, perhaps an arm and a head too.

874   You know what Navy Coach Eddie Erdelatz said about a tie: "It has all the thrill of kissing your sister."

875   George Allen says winning can be defined as the reward of being totally prepared. I think we can agree that the team was as totally prepared as any team could be. Certainly much credit should go to Coach . . .

876   As the fictional character Tom Brown said in *Tom Brown's School Days* about cricket, "It's more than a game; it's an institution." And in the same way one could say that professional football now is an institution—a part of our lives. . . .

877   When Paul Waner, former Pittsburgh Pirate outfielder, was asked how he knew when it was time to quit baseball, he replied: "Well, as you get older, you slow down and the infielders back up because they've got more time to throw you out at first. At the same time you lose a little power, so the outfielders move in, since you're not hitting the ball so far. When they can shake hands, you've had it." That just about describes my decision.

878   As Yogi Berra said, "There are some people who if they don't already know, you can't tell them." And people should know by now who has been the source of inspiration for this team.

879   When Manager Red Rolfe of the Detroit Tigers was asked why he hired the old veteran Yankee Charlie Keller to join the team, he replied, "I didn't hire Charlie Keller because he was a Yankee or because we're friends or because I wanted to do him a favor. I hired him because I wanted to give the ball club a touch of class." Well, we can all agree that one person who has brought a touch of class to this team is . . .

880   In *This Side of Paradise,* F. Scott Fitzgerald wrote: "Life was a damned muddle . . . a football game with every one off-side and the referee gotten rid of—every one claiming the referee would have been on his side."

881   André Maurois wrote, "Business is a combination of war and sport."

882   As John Kennedy once said, "We are inclined to think that if we watch a football game or a baseball game we have taken part in it."

883   As Branch Rickey once said, "Luck is the residue of design."

884   One of the lessons we athletes learn is how to adapt. Some years ago when Coach Otto Graham of the Washington Redskins asked his quarterback Sonny Jurgensen how his injured right arm felt (Jurgensen with an ailing arm had thrown five touchdown passes against the Chicago Bears): "What are you going to do about it?" Jurgensen replied, "Drink left-handed."

885   I am glad that we didn't follow the Aztec tradition. In their game of ball the leader of the losing team was sacrificed to the sun.

886   Joe Louis put it bluntly when he was interviewed before his second fight with Billy Conn. Asked how he would handle Conn's back-pedaling tactics in the ring, he simply said, "He can run, but he can't hide." We can run from the social problems of our times. But we can't hide. This is not a time for running or hiding.

887   Once Manager Leo Durocher brought up a young outfielder from the minors to play for the Cubs. When the Cubs got well ahead in the game, he put the rookie in center field. He promptly dropped a fly ball, made a wild throw, and the game was tied. Durocher pulled out the rookie and put in a veteran in center field. But the veteran dropped a fly and the other side won. Enraged, Durocher grabbed the rookie on the bench and shouted, "You've got center field so screwed up no one can play it."

888   New York Yankees manager Joe McCarthy once said in regard to Ted Williams, "Any manager who can't get along with a .400 hitter is crazy."

889   Tommy Henrich of the New York Yankees once commented that "catching a fly ball is a pleasure but knowing what to do with it is a business."

890   Regarding ability, Casey Stengel said it is "the art of getting credit for all the home runs somebody else hits."

891   Russell Baker commented on sports in America in the *New York Times,* "In America, it is sport that is the opiate of the masses."

892   I am reminded only too well of the truth in what Frank Gifford said, "Pro football is like nuclear warfare. There are no winners, only survivors."

893   The first Olympic races started in 870 B.C. The old ridged stone starting tracks are still extant today. In the days of ancient Greece, the highest honor one could bestow on a young man was the privilege of carrying the torch in the procession toward the Olympic games. But it was a responsibility as well as a privilege—the responsibility to hold high and keep alight the flame in the annual Olympic pageant, as the finest Greek athletes underwent the supreme physical ordeal.

STATESMAN

894   President Eisenhower once said, "In 1776 our forefathers started a revolution that still goes on."

895   In his First Inaugural Address, President Eisenhower said, "Whatever America hopes to bring to pass in this world must first come to pass in the heart of America."

896   When Joseph Martin of Massachusetts was Speaker of the House, he was fond of recalling the note a woman wrote to the editor of her local newspaper, "I want to get into politics. Do the taxpayers have a party?" To which the editor replied, "Very seldom, lady, very seldom."

897   At least twice in his life Sigmund Freud observed that there were three "impossible professions: educating, healing and governing." In the end Freud did not believe that man would succeed in controlling "the human instinct of aggression and self-destruction."

898   The new social legislation which has been designed to shore up the body politic leads me curiously enough to Michelangelo. When the great master had concluded his painting on the ceiling of the Sistine Chapel in Rome, he feared that time would crumble the walls and destroy his work. He appealed to the Pope to shore up the building with brick supports to prevent the ultimate catastrophe. The Pope, not unmindful of the eccentricities of genius, refused the request. Thereupon Michelangelo mounted the scaffold and painted in cracks so realistic that when the Pope came to view the painting again he was horrified at his own neglect. He immediately authorized the expenditure for the brick supports. They can be seen today shoring up the walls; so can the painted cracks, which have been left as a testimonial to Michelangelo's realism and imaginativeness combined. Anyone who has been privileged to gaze at that ceiling and be filled with beauty as if the sky itself were there, will not regret the precaution taken by the master or even the deception with which he preserved his art. Well, today we must also paint in alarming cracks if we are to arouse the people to shore up their democracies and preserve them for the future.

899   In Richard Crossman's memoirs the Labourite M.P. tells of a Cabinet meeting with Prime Minister Harold Wilson. After an issue was discussed around the table, there was a vote. When it came to the Prime Minister, the vote was nine to nine. Wilson turned to Crossman and said, "How should I vote—it's a tie?" "Be a Prime Minister," said Crossman.

900   Warren Harding's father once told him, "Warren, it's a good thing you weren't born a gal . . . you'd be in the family way all the time. You can't say 'No.' "

901   Franklin Delano Roosevelt once said, "The basic things expected by our people of their political and economic systems are simple. They are: Equality of opportunity for youth and others. Jobs for those who can work. Security for those who need it. The ending of special privilege for the few. The preser-

vation of civil liberties for all. The enjoyment of the fruits of scientific progress in a wider and constantly rising standard of living."

902   Henry Kissinger once defined the problem of government: "For the spirit of policy and that of bureaucracy are diametrically opposed. The essence of policy is its contingency; its success depends on the correctness of an estimate which is in part conjectural. The essence of bureaucracy is its quest for safety; its success is calculability. Profound policy thrives on perpetual creation, on a constant redefinition of goals. Good administration thrives on routine, the definition of relationships which can survive mediocrity. Policy involves an adjustment of risks; administration an avoidance of deviation."

903   I realize as De Tocqueville said over 135 years ago, "There are many men of principle in both parties in America, but there is no party of principle."

904   In *Profiles in Courage,* John F. Kennedy wrote, "The question is how we will compromise and with whom. For it is easy to seize upon unnecessary concessions, not as means of legitimately resolving conflicts but as methods of 'going along.' "

905   In 1960 the commentator Richard Harkness wrote this about the presidential campaign: "When it comes to serious problems, each candidate will pledge to appoint a committee. And what is a committee? A group of the unwilling picked from the unfit, to do the unnecessary. But it all sounds great in a campaign speech."

906   During one of his Fireside Chats, Franklin Delano Roosevelt said, "We build and defend not for our generation alone. We defend the foundations laid by our fathers. We build a life for generations yet unborn. We defend and we build a way of life, not for America alone, but for all mankind."

907   When leaders of the emergent Republican party suggested during the war to President Lincoln that it tone down

its opposition to slavery, the Great Emancipator replied: "The Republican party should not become a mere sucked egg, all shell and no meat, the principle all sucked out."

908   Dwight D. Eisenhower delivered a speech to Columbia University, October 12, 1948. In it he said: "The common responsibility of all Americans is to become effective, helpful participants in a way of life that blends and harmonizes the fiercely competitive demands of the individual and of society. The individual must be free, able to develop to the utmost of his ability, employing all opportunities that confront him for his own and his family's welfare; otherwise he is merely a cog in a machine. The society must be stable, assured against violent upheaval and revolution; otherwise it is nothing but a temporary truce with chaos. But freedom for the individual must never degenerate into the brutish struggle for survival that we call barbarism. Neither must the stability of society ever degenerate into the enchained servitude of the masses that we call statism."

909   When the Constitutional Convention had completed its deliberations, and the draft of the document had been finished and approved, Americans were anxious to learn the new frame of government. For weeks, the delegates had met in closed session; now the sessions were over. As the delegates filed out, one student met Benjamin Franklin on the steps of the chamber.

"Dr. Franklin, what type of government did you give us?" Franklin replied, "A republic, if you can keep it."

910   In the world's first democracy of Athens the Greeks had a word for those intellectual members of society who refused to participate in the realm of public affairs. They described those who criticized but disdained engagement in the political process as "unwhole people," incomplete men or half citizens. The actual greek word was "idiot." Today Americans who condemn the evils of society but who refuse to use the tools of democratic change may also be called "idiots."

911   In his farewell address of March 4, 1837, Andrew Jackson said: "You have the highest of human trusts committed to your care. Providence has showered on this favored land blessings without number and has chosen you as the guardians of freedom, to preserve it for the benefit of the human race. May he who holds in his hands the destinies of nations make you worthy of the favors he has bestowed and enable you, with pure hearts and pure hands and sleepless vigilance, to guard and defend to the end of time the charge he has committed to your keeping."

912   In 1825, General Lafayette made a nostalgic trip back to the country whose independence he helped secure. Anxious to see how this experiment in self-government was making out, he toured the cities and towns of the emerging republic. In January, 1826, he wrote to a colleague and French general these words, which evinced his faith in the American democracy: "They are solving the magnificent problem of liberty."

913   Once when Henry Clay was driving back from Washington in a stagecoach, a friend asked him if he was supporting his American plan for internal improvements. At the next stop, Clay got out of the coach and put his ear down to the ground and told his friend to do likewise. When his companion claimed he didn't hear anything, Clay replied, "I do—I hear the tread of the unborn millions." Let us when we legislate and administrate hear those unborn millions and let us secure for them their coming birthright into a free America and free world.

914   Demosthenes, the great Athenian statesman, was asked why the citizenry of Athens failed to rally against the dictatorship of Philip of Macedon. Demosthenes blamed the leaders for failing to tell the truth to the people: they did not dare to ask the citizenry to make the sacrifices as they had so valiantly in the past: "If you analyze the problem correctly, you will conclude that the critical problem is chiefly due to those who try to please the citizens rather than tell them what they need to hear."

915   In 1848 the French writer Alexis de Tocqueville feared the effects of the arising turbulence in the French nation. As a Deputy in the French Chamber he called upon French political leaders to look into their own hearts. In his closing phrases he said, "In such times as these you are remaining calm before the degradation of public morality. You are speaking of legislative changes and I believe they are necessary. I believe in the need of electoral reform, in the urgency of parliamentary reform . . . but it is not the mechanics of laws that produces great events, gentlemen, but the inner spirit of governments." Today we say that it is not the American people who have lost sight of our American dream and our national purpose. It is the political leadership who often lose sight of the American spirit and forget those qualities of initiative, self-destiny, and resolution that made our country great.

STATISTICIAN

916   The problem with us statisticians is that too often we use statistics as drunks use lampposts—for support rather than illumination. But I think the following statistics about recent shifts in population . . .

917   "Statistics," said Mark Twain, "are like ladies of the night. Once you get them down, you can do anything with them." But recently all the leading polls agree that . . .

STUDENT LEADER

918   The life of a young person today is tough and confusing. Most of his early years are spent listening to someone tell him to get lost. When he begins to grow up, everybody puts pressure on him to start finding himself. But I think as we look back over the past few years each of us has gotten to know himself a little better.

919   A young person can consider himself educated, not when he receives a diploma for completing school, but when he arrives at that point in life when he stops answering questions and begins questioning the answers. Today I would like to begin by questioning a few of the myths that have been handed to us as veritable truths.

920   As Prime Minister William Pitt once said, "The atrocious crime of being a young man . . . I shall neither attempt to palliate nor deny." And similarly we won't apologize for our inexperience when we have not been offered the chance to find our mission or even make our own mistakes.

921   Alfred North Whitehead said, "Celibacy does not suit a university; it must mate itself with action." That is why we as students cannot pretend to ignore the injustice . . .

922   In July, 1969, a law student, Melvin E. Levine, told the adult generation at his Harvard graduation: "You have given us our visions and then asked us to curb them. You have offered us dreams and then urged us to abandon them. You have made us idealists and then told us to go slowly." Well, the time for going slowly is past. The time for accepting token measures is past. We are impatient with injustice. That is why we offer today this plan of action.

923   When the former Czech leader Alexander Dubcek was asked by protesting Prague students what was the best guarantee of a free and progressive government, he replied, "You are that guarantee. You, the youth of our country are that guarantee." Today we must ask ourselves if we are living up to that warrant. Have we the discipline and decisiveness to be the cutting edge for change?

924   As Robert Louis Stevenson said, "Give me the young man who has enough brains to make a fool of himself."

925   Mohammed once wrote that the ink of the scholar is more sacred than the blood of a martyr.

926   Of his education Henry Adams once remarked: "Four years of Harvard College, if successful, resulted in an autobiographical blank, a mind on which only a watermark had been stamped."

927   Thomas Carlyle designed a book plate which expresses the idealism of students, "I burn that I may be of use."

TEACHER

928   As I look out over my former pupils, I think of old Mr. Chips—James Hilton's schoolmaster. Someone once said, "Pity he had no children." "Oh, but I have," he replied, "Thousands of them and all boys." Like Mr. Chips, I have had many children —students who have enriched my life and given me far more than I have ever given them.

929   In Robert Anderson's book *After* the headmaster says, "My fondest hope is that while you develop the minds of men you will retain the hearts of boys." In another sense we could say we are searching for idealists who have shed their illusions and realists who have shed their ideals.

930   Near the turn of the century when Benjamin Jowett, the Oxford professor, asked one of his students what his aspirations were, the student said, "To find the Holy Grail." "But," asked Jowett, "when you find the Holy Grail, what are you going to do then?" The university cannot be used as a refuge —as a shelter away from social responsibilities.

931   It was George Bernard Shaw who said, "He who can, does. He who cannot, teaches." That may explain how I got into teaching—but it does not express all the satisfaction . . .

932   Henry Adams wrote, "A teacher affects eternity; he can never tell where his influence stops." And no one can measure the influence my colleague has had . . .

933   When the husband of Alice Freeman Palmer, president of Wellesley, asked her why she didn't retire and devote some time to study and scholarship, she replied, "It is people who count—I like putting myself into people." And getting into the hearts and minds of students is what education is all about.

934   In *The Prime of Miss Jean Brodie* the teacher-heroine says to her Scottish pupils, "Little girls, I am in the business of putting old heads on young shoulders, and all my pupils are the crème de la crème. Give me a girl at an impressionable age, and she is mine for life."

935   Jacques Barzun once said, "Teaching is not a lost art, but the regard for it is a lost tradition." Tonight we hope to help restore that tradition by honoring . . .

936   Since Henry Adams wrote that "nothing is more tiresome than a superannuated pedagogue," I will be brief in my remarks.

937   In the play *A Man for All Seasons* Sir Thomas More tries to convince Richards to go into teaching instead of politics. "But," Richards objects, "who would know it?" "You would", replied More. "Be a teacher."

938   Henry David Thoreau, when asked if he had traveled much, replied, "I have traveled widely in Concord."

TRUSTEE

939   As Solomon wrote, "Remove not the ancient landmarks which your fathers have set."

940   In frontier days there was the ceremony of the peacestone—home owners put a piece of glass in the newel post of the house to signify the mortgage was paid off.

941   The first piece of land General Eisenhower ever owned was the farm he bought in Gettysburg after World War II. When he was asked by the recording clerk in the Gettysburg

courthouse at the time of settlement why he wanted to have property, he replied, "When I die, I want to leave a piece of ground better than I found it."

URBAN LEADER

942   T. S. Eliot wrote, "When the stranger says: 'What is the meaning of this city? Do you huddle close together because you love each other?' What will you answer? 'We all dwell together to make money from each other'? or 'This is a community'?"

943   A strong America depends on its cities—America's glory and sometimes America's shame.

URBAN PLANNER

944   In *Nobody Knows My Name,* James Baldwin wrote, "A ghetto can be improved in one way only; out of existence."

945   Aristotle noted that "a very populous city can rarely, if ever, be well governed."

946   I am reminded today of the words of E. B. White when he said, "Commuters give the city its tidal restlessness; natives give it solidity and continuity; but the settlers give it passion."

947   As the famous planner Daniel Burnham once wrote, "Make no little plans; they have no magic to stir men's blood." Today I think we have a plan that will stir the soul of the audience and one that will make the city come alive.

948   One of the oldest municipal problems is that of sanitation. In Thebes in Egypt in 2500 B.C. the officials wanted the citizens to empty their waste in strategically-placed cisterns outside the city walls. The citizens preferred to dump it in back of their own dwellings. Today we face a similar problem in

transportation—people would rather have the convenience of a car than the safety and economy of mass transit.

949   City problems are not new. In the fourth century B.C. the Greek orator Isocrates wrote, "Athens is a great place but I wouldn't want to live there." Our challenge today is to make our city a great place in which to live as well as to work or play.

950   In his farewell to Philadelphia, William Penn, before sailing back to England, wrote this prayer, "And thou Philadelphia, virgin settlement of this province named before thou wert born, what love, what care, what service, and what travail have there been to bring thee forth and preserve thee from such as would abuse and defile thee." Today it is appropriate to honor those in this city who have given service, care, and even love.

951   In 1770 Robert Crowley wrote this poem about London and the lack of concern,

> And this is a city
> In name, but in deed
> It is a pack of people
> That seek after meed
> For officers and all
> Do seek their own gain
> But for the wealth of the Commons
> Not one taketh pain
> And hell without order
> I may it well call
> Where every man is for himself
> And no man for all.

952   The urban planner Edward Logue has said, "The city is not obsolete; it's the center of our civilization." Today I would like to talk on ways to improve our city as a center for work, for recreation, for the arts.

953   As John Kennedy said to Congress in 1962, "We will neglect our cities to our peril, for in neglecting them we neglect the nation."

VICTOR

954   As tonight's victor my wife has reminded me, amid all the congratulations, of how in the Roman days a hero, after a victory, was given a triumph—an affair of state. As he was borne by chariot heading a stream of parading soldiers and civil officers, a person by law had to ride behind him in a chariot chanting in his ear, "Now remember, don't let it go to your head—you're not invincible."

WIFE

955   When someone asked me before the anniversary reception tonight whether I ever contemplated divorce, I repeated Lillian Hellman's line in the play *Autumn Garden* answering the same question: "Divorce, never—murder, often." But seriously . . .

956   Somerset Maugham once said American women expect to find in their husbands a perfection that English women only hope to find in their butlers. And I would like to add that I found not only someone who mixes a wicked martini but also someone who is pretty perfect in other ways.

WINNER

957   It is a great thing to win but I can't help but remember what Woodrow Wilson once said about those elected to significant office. He said those who take office either grow or swell. Well, I am going to watch myself carefully to see whether I am swelling or growing.

WRITER

958   As Ernest Hemingway wrote to Carlos Baker, "The good and the bad, the ecstasy, the remorse and sorrow, the people and the places and how the weather was. If you can get so that you can give that to people, then you are a writer." And the man we honor tonight fits that definition in every respect.

959   Rudyard Kipling had this formula for fiction, "Know your subject well—then distort."

Index of Subjects

*References to numbered anecdotes and role bits are given in **bold face**.*

Index of Names